This Do in
Remembrance of Me

This Do in Remembrance of Me

by Arie Elshout

Translated by
Bartel Elshout

REFORMATION HERITAGE BOOKS
Grand Rapids, Michigan

Published by

REFORMATION HERITAGE BOOKS
2965 Leonard St., NE
Grand Rapids, MI 49525
616-977-0889 / Fax 616-285-3246
e-mail: orders@heritagebooks.org
website: www.heritagebooks.org

Library of Congress Cataloging-in-Publication Data

Elshout, Arie, 1923-1991.
  [Doet dat tot Mijn gedachtenis. English]
  This do in remembrance of Me / by Arie Elshout ; translated by Bartel
Elshout.
    p. cm.
  ISBN 978-1-60178-080-5 (pbk. : alk. paper)
  1. Lord's Supper—Reformed Church. 2. Forgiveness of sin. 3.
Reformed Church—Doctrines. I. Title.
  BX9423.C5E4713 2010
  264'.042492036--dc22
                                            2009049053

---

*For additional Reformed literature, both new and used, request a
free book list from Reformation Heritage Books at the above address.*

Table of Contents

Preface

The title of this book relates to the manner in which we are to be exercised with the Lord's Supper, and is derived from the words of the Lord Jesus when He instituted the Holy Supper (Luke 22:19b).

The words, "This do in remembrance of me," are a loving command. In issuing them, the Lord did not only have His glory in mind. By instituting the Lord's Supper and mandating its use, the Lord also had the well-being of His people in mind. By their partaking of His Supper, it pleases the Lord to instruct and strengthen His people in the crucible of this life. The Lord knows our frame and He remembers that we are dust (Ps. 103:14). He knows that His people are so inclined to cast the anchor of their hope in the wrong place. He knows how distressed and anxious they can be when they reflect on the past, the present, and the future. So often they are grieved and troubled because of their sins.

The Lord desires to bless those who are afflicted and tossed with tempest (Isa. 54:11). He said to Isaiah, "Comfort ye, comfort ye my people, saith your God. Speak ye comfortably to Jerusalem, and cry unto her, that her warfare is accomplished, that her iniquity is pardoned: for she hath received of the LORD's hand double for all her sins" (Isa. 40:1–2). This message of comfort is signified and sealed in the Lord's Supper in a visible, tangible, and sacramental manner.

The broken bread and poured-out wine point to the foundation on which the comforting message of forgiveness and divine provision rests. That foundation is reconciliation on the basis of the accomplished work of Him who "by one offering...hath perfected for ever them that are sanctified" (Heb. 10:14). The work of the Lord Jesus Christ, which includes His active and passive obedience, is the ground upon which we must cast the anchor of our hope—and nowhere else.

The words, "This do in remembrance of me," command us to be exercised by the Lord's Supper. They for whom the Lord has instituted His Supper can struggle to obey this commandment of love. Doubt as to whether we belong to the Lord's people and fear of eating and drinking the body and blood of the Lord unworthily, frequently prompt some to refrain from partaking whom the Lord desires to comfort and refresh with the bread and wine.

The motivation for writing this book is to extend a helping hand to those who are sorry for their sins (Ps. 38:19). To facilitate the reflection and the discussion of the subject matter of this book both at home and beyond, a number of questions have been added to each chapter. May the Lord bless the discussion of the contents of this book so that the words of Psalter 373:7 (Psalm 135) will be understood and practiced:

> *Thy Name shall abide, O Jehovah,*
> *Through all generations renowned;*
> *The Lord is the judge of His people,*
> *His mercies forever abound.*

—1—
God's Loving Provision

The testimony of the Lord recorded in Exodus 3, where we read the Spirit-inspired account of how the Lord appeared to Moses in the midst of the burning bush, is a touching one indeed. After the Lord directed Moses to remove his shoes because of the holy ground on which he stood, He told him about the impending deliverance of the people of Israel. In verses 6–10, the Lord says to Moses,

> I am the God of thy father, the God of Abraham, the God of Isaac, and the God of Jacob. And Moses hid his face; for he was afraid to look upon God. And the LORD said, I have surely seen the affliction of my people which are in Egypt, and have heard their cry by reason of their taskmasters; for I know their sorrows; and I am come down to deliver them out of the hand of the Egyptians, and to bring them up out of that land unto a good land and a large, unto a land flowing with milk and honey; unto the place of the Canaanites, and the Hittites, and the Amorites, and the Perizzites, and the Hivites, and the Jebusites. Now therefore, behold, the cry of the children of Israel is come unto me: and I have also seen the oppression wherewith the Egyptians oppress them. Come now therefore, and I will send thee unto Pharaoh, that thou mayest bring forth my people the children of Israel out of Egypt.

Stephen, moved by the Holy Spirit, paraphrased this passage in his address to the Sanhedrin: "Then said the

Lord to him (Moses)…I have seen the affliction of my people which is in Egypt, and I have heard their groaning, and am come down to deliver them. And now come, I will send thee into Egypt" (Acts 7:34).

In commissioning Moses, the Lord first gave him a message for the oppressed children of Israel. We read of this in Exodus 3:15–17:

> And God said moreover unto Moses, Thus shalt thou say unto the children of Israel, The LORD God of your fathers, the God of Abraham, the God of Isaac, and the God of Jacob, hath sent me unto you: this is my name for ever, and this is my memorial unto all generations. Go, and gather the elders of Israel together, and say unto them, The LORD God of your fathers, the God of Abraham, of Isaac, and of Jacob, appeared unto me, saying, I have surely visited you, and seen that which is done to you in Egypt: and I have said, I will bring you up out of the affliction of Egypt unto the land of the Canaanites, and the Hittites, and the Amorites, and the Perizzites, and the Hivites, and the Jebusites, unto a land flowing with milk and honey.

Moses was also commanded to say to the children of Israel that the "I AM" had sent him to them. The essential meaning of the name Jehovah, whereby the Lord revealed Himself for the first time to Moses, is *that God is who He says He is and does what He promises He will do.* Furthermore, Moses was also told to give Pharaoh the message that he should let the oppressed people of Israel go to the place of the Lord's choosing. Finally, Moses received the gift to perform signs and wonders before the eyes of Israel (as a confirmation of God's Word and promises), as well as before the eyes of Pharaoh, in order to bring about the deliverance of His oppressed people. By God's effectual grace, Moses faithfully performed this task, proclaiming many messages in the name of the Lord to the despairing and fearful Israelites—the church militant—as well as to a stiffnecked Pharaoh. He performed many encouraging signs for the weeping and sighing Israelites, and by the power of God he inflicted dreadful plagues on the Egyptians.

Before the actual deliverance of Israel was accomplished, the Lord commanded Moses to celebrate the Passover. That Passover meal was a sign and seal of the covenant of grace, the same covenant the Lord remembered when He heard the groanings of the children of Israel (Ex. 2:23). The Passover visibly confirmed to the children of Israel that their impending deliverance was not attributed to any worthiness found in them, but was exclusively because of God's grace and faithfulness. The angel of death would pass over the houses of the Israelites solely on the basis of substitution. A lamb had to be slain in the place of people who were worthy of being slain because of their sins. Because of sin, the children of Israel (represented by their firstborn) were children of wrath. Only when the blood of the Paschal Lamb was applied by faith to the posts of the doors would the angel of death (God's messenger of wrath) pass over the houses of the Israelites.

They were delivered from the sword of the angel of death not because they were children of the covenant, but because they took refuge in the blood of the covenant. The Passover would be to Israel what circumcision was to Abraham: a sign and seal of the righteousness of faith (Rom. 4:11). In Genesis 15:6 we read, "And he (Abraham) believed in the LORD; and he counted it to him for righteousness." Abraham was not righteous before God *because* of his faith, but rather, his faith was *counted* unto him as righteousness.

Abraham was constituted righteous before God only by the imputation of Christ's perfect righteousness. Abraham's faith was not perfect, and thus his faith could never be the meriting cause of his righteousness before God. The

fact that Abraham's faith was counted to him as righteousness was the fruit of Christ's mediatorial work and an act of
God's grace. For Abraham and all believers, being counted
righteous and living by faith (rather than perishing because
of our sins) is completely attributable to God's sovereign
favor, good pleasure, and tender mercy (Luke 1:78).

The Passover visibly taught the people of Israel these
truths, just as these truths are now visibly displayed to us
in the Lord's Supper. The Passover and the Lord's Supper
point us to Christ, the Lamb of God, who has taken away
the sins of the world, and whose blood cleanses from all
sin. Circumcision and the Passover, as well as Baptism and
the Lord's Supper, signify and seal the words of the Lord
Jesus Christ: "God so loved the world, that he gave his only
begotten Son, that whosoever believeth in him should not
perish, but have everlasting life" (John 3:16).

God's Word and the sacraments of the Old and New
Testament have been instituted to instruct us that faith in
the sacrifice of Jesus Christ on the cross is the only foundation of our salvation. And, indeed it is, "for the Holy Ghost
teaches us in the gospel, and assures us by the sacraments,
that the whole of our salvation [i.e., of true believers] depends upon that one sacrifice of Christ which He offered
for us on the cross" (Heidelberg Catechism, Q. 67).

In both his person and work, Moses was a figure of
Christ who came to seek and to save that which is lost.
In Moses' labor on behalf of the suffering Israelites shines
forth the work of Him of whom we read in Psalm 72:12–14:
"He shall deliver the needy when he crieth; the poor also,
and him that hath no helper. He shall spare the poor and
needy, and shall save the souls of the needy. He shall re-
deem their soul from deceit and violence: and precious
shall their blood be in his sight."

Thus far I have pointed out to you the similarities
between the Passover and the Lord's Supper. There are,

however, also differences. The Passover was a bloody sacrament, whereas the Lord's Supper is not. The Passover pointed Israel to a Christ, a Redeemer, who would come; the Lord's Supper points us to the Christ who has come. The Passover pointed to the sacrifice of Christ that would be offered in the future. The Lord's Supper reflects on the sacrifice of Christ which has been accomplished and by which He has "perfected forever them that are sanctified" (Heb. 10:14).

Another noteworthy difference is that all Israelites took part of the Passover according to the divinely instituted stipulations. When we turn to the New Testament and consider for whom the Lord's Supper was instituted, it is evident that its objective is to strengthen the faith of true believers. In order to eat the Passover, it was sufficient to be a member of the Old Testament church and to be ceremonially clean. However, in order to partake of the Lord's Supper, it is expressly required that one be born again, be united to Christ, be grafted into Him by a true faith—and thus be truly converted.

These are very significant differences! The Lord Himself, the Author of the Holy Scriptures, has made these distinctions. Both the external and internal relationships to this covenant—not just the external—are prerequisites to partake at the Lord's Table in a manner that is pleasing to God. Under no circumstances may we tamper with this! Anyone who does will have to deal with the Lord who said that whoever eats and drinks unworthily is eating and drinking judgment unto himself. In preparation for the Lord's Supper, God's faithful servants will apply the biblical marks of saving faith as they instruct the congregation.

This essential separation between true, Spirit-wrought faith and counterfeit faith is of the utmost importance. Many deem such separation unnecessary. They even condemn it, wishing to be wiser than God. They place themselves above God who deems it necessary to instruct His servants accordingly, giving numerous touchstones in the Holy Scriptures whereby we can examine ourselves so that we would not eat or drink judgment to ourselves, not discerning the Lord's body.

Anyone who has an aversion for self-examination renders himself very suspect. The saints in Scripture had no such aversion. One needs but read the Psalms to affirm this. They were so fearful of self-deception and desired to know from the Lord Himself whether they deceived themselves—whether there was any evil way within them. In giving a scriptural response to the question for whom the Lord's Supper was instituted, the authors of the Heidelberg Catechism have drawn clear and scriptural lines of demarcation in Question 81. Those same lines of demarcation were drawn by the authors of the Form for the Administration of the Lord's Supper.

In their exposition and application of Question 81, the Reformers and ministers of the Dutch Further Reformation, including Justus Vermeer, were zealous in instructing the churches regarding this important question. They emphatically stated that an ecclesiastical right to partake of the Lord's Supper (which all professing members of a church who are not under Christian discipline do have) is not sufficient by itself to partake worthily. Without tampering with the ecclesiastical duty of all professing members of the congregation to be worthy partakers of the sacraments, rooted in the fourth commandment (cf. Heidelberg Catechism, Q. 103), our forefathers argued that in addition to an ecclesiastical right there must also be a filial right. When He instituted the Lord's Supper, the Lord gave this filial right exclusively to His children, saying, "This do in remembrance of me."

Though many books have been published by godly authors that specifically address sensitive and searching questions regarding the celebration of the Lord's Supper, there are still many reoccurring problems that call for a detailed response.

The second touchstone for self-examination, articulated in the Form for the Administration of the Lord's Supper, is particularly confusing for many of the godly and proves to be a stumbling block that either hinders them from partaking of the Lord's Supper or at least makes it very difficult for them. Due to ignorance of Satan's devices, the following paragraph has become a stumbling block for many:

> *Secondly.* That every one examine his own heart whether he doth believe this faithful promise of God that all his sins are forgiven him only for the sake of the passion and death of Jesus Christ, and that the perfect righteousness of Christ is imputed and freely given him as his own, yea, so perfectly, as if he had satisfied in his own person for all his sins and fulfilled all righteousness.[1]

Though this sacrament is given by the Lord to strengthen the faith of His church—a faith so pointedly articulated in the Belgic Confession of Faith—some entirely neglect this sacrament as they experience the great strife that accompanies the true life of faith. For others, due to spiritual confusion and uncertainty about what is required by this second touchstone, the use of the sacrament does not yield the fruit which it would yield with the Lord's blessing if they had a better insight into what our forefathers intended to say in this paragraph. In the next chapter, we shall focus on this in more detail.

---

1. All quotations from the Form for the Administration of the Lord's Supper are from *Doctrinal Standards, Liturgy, and Church Order*, ed. Joel R. Beeke (Grand Rapids; Reformation Heritage Books, 1999) 136–40.

Discussion Questions

1. Who should be exercised regarding the partaking of the Lord's Supper?

2. In considering the Lord's Supper, what should be at the forefront of our minds: God's loving command or our need?

3. How are the meaning and the use of the Passover and the Lord's Supper similar and dissimilar?

4. There is a relationship between Baptism, public Profession of Faith, and partaking of the Lord's Supper, and there are differences in one's participation in these covenant events. What is this relationship, and what are the differences?

5. Should professing members of the congregation be commended for not partaking of the Lord's Supper?

2

Read Carefully What It Says!

An important factor in misunderstanding what our fathers intended to say in the second touchstone for self-examination—given so that we may "celebrate the Supper of the Lord to our comfort"—is the incorrect reading of the Form for the Administration of the Lord's Supper.

The biography of the late Rev. M. Heikoop tells something regarding this matter which can also be to our edification.[1] His first partaking of the Lord's Supper (before he was a minister) turned out so very differently than he had anticipated. He was cold, void of feeling, and without any impression regarding the matter at hand. There was not the least trace of the unction of the Spirit. Consequently, he found his soul enveloped in thick darkness.

Until that moment, he had always been of the opinion that a person had to have full assurance of faith in order to partake of the Lord's Supper. We understand the full assurance of faith to mean that a believer is fully conscious of being righteous before God and an heir of eternal life. But according to Heikoop, the believer needed to possess this full consciousness in order to partake at the Table of the Covenant. He was convinced that this conclusion was derived from the Form for the Lord's Supper, which states

---

1. Rev. M. Heikoop (1880–1944) served as pastor of the Gereformeerde Gemeente of Utrecht, The Netherlands. For the benefit of those who do not possess this commendable little book, I will extract a few passages from pp. 48–50 that tell about his first partaking of the Lord's Supper.

that he must "believe this faithful promise of God that all his sins are forgiven him only for the sake of the passion and death of Jesus Christ," etc.

Even though Heikoop had been a partaker of the life of grace for many years, he had never participated in the celebration of the Lord's Supper. He had, however, been present several times when this sacrament had been administered in church, and when he saw some of the Lord's concerned people approach the table, he would inwardly oppose their going to the table. In his judgment, they were taking this step too soon.

For himself, however, matters were now different. He could apply the words of Romans 5:1 to himself: "Therefore being justified by faith, we have peace with God through our Lord Jesus Christ." He could share the language of Paul: "For I know whom I have believed" (2 Tim. 1:12). But after having attended the Lord's Supper for the first time, and finding it so disappointing, he thought that perhaps all was wrong with him.

In the days following the Lord's Supper, his experience at the table led to serious self-examination. It pleased the Lord to shed light on the cause of this fruitless first partaking. The Lord first of all showed him that true preparation had been lacking, and consequently, he had approached the Lord's Table in a haughty spiritual frame. Had there been preparation, he would have come to the Lord's Table as a penitent sinner rather than as a justified man.

As genuine as his experience of justification was, it was not the basis on which he should have attended. The purpose of the Lord's Supper did not consist in the commemoration of his own justification, but rather, of the precious suffering and death of the Lord Jesus Christ. In his foolishness, he had put more stock in his faith than in the finished work of Christ. He now learned to understand that he could not be acceptable with God by virtue of the worthiness of his faith, even though he had received it in a larger measure than before. Faith was but the necessary hand to appropriate the imputation of Christ and His righteousness as being the true basis for partaking of the Lord's Supper. He had partaken of the sacrament as a worthy subject rather than an unworthy subject, and therefore the Lord concealed Himself at the Table.

Another reason he perceived why the Lord had not manifested Himself to his soul was to expose his erroneous view that he must be consciously assured of his state of grace before partaking of the Lord's Supper. If the Lord would have acquiesced in this, how it would have reaffirmed his error! Consequently, he would have become a haughty and unapproachable man for truly concerned souls. He would have been in danger of establishing his view as a benchmark for others. He would have been guilty of oppressing the weak, particularly in his labors as an office-bearer, and of grieving those souls whom God desires to comfort, for although every regenerate person must persistently endeavor to grow in grace, the Lord is nevertheless free to deal to every man the measure of faith as pleases Him (Rom. 12:3). His eyes were opened to the fact that for years he had read the Form as follows: "... whether he doth *assuredly* believe this promise of God," rather than, as it is written, "...whether he doth believe this *faithful* promise of God."

For years I also read this passage of the form incorrectly, and in my ministry I have encountered many who, in spite of much instruction, also entertain a wrong notion about this. As I sought to instruct others regarding this, I have heard countless times, "But Pastor, does the Form not say that we must assuredly believe that our sins are forgiven, and that the righteousness of Christ is our own so that it is as if I had accomplished all righteousness myself?"

Upon my reply, "That is not what it says," they would

look at me in great disbelief. We would then consult the Form for the Lord's Supper, and, with utter amazement, they read that they had been in error. Satan always twists words and matters in order to mislead and confuse us, and is certainly not without blame when it comes to our misunderstanding this passage of the Form for the Lord's Supper.

The authors of the form did *not* state that the worthy partaker of the Lord's Supper is someone who, among other things, believes God's promises *assuredly*. Rather, they have said the following: "That every one examine his own heart whether he doth believe this faithful promise of God that all his sins are forgiven him only for the sake of the passion and death of Jesus Christ, and that the perfect righteousness of Christ is imputed and freely given him as his own, yea, so perfectly, as if he had satisfied in his own person for all his sins and fulfilled all righteousness." This harmonizes with what is asked in Question 81 of the Heidelberg Catechism, "For whom is the Lord's Supper instituted? For those who are truly sorrowful for their sins, and yet trust that these are forgiven them for the sake of Christ; and that their remaining infirmities are covered by His passion and death...."

Neither the authors of the Heidelberg Catechism nor of the Form for the Lord's Supper intended to say that we must possess the full assurance of faith to be worthy partakers of the Lord's Supper in God's sight. Regarding the authors of the Heidelberg Catechism, it is evident (according to the judgment of countless divines) that in Lord's Day 7 they are not defining the quintessence of faith, but rather, its essence.

If someone asks what the difference is between the essence and the quintessence of faith, I will explain this by way of a simple example. Let us consider a newborn baby boy. In his essence, he is a man. If everything is normal, he will possess everything he will need to function as a man upon reaching maturity. Being a full-grown man is the quintessence of manhood. A healthy baby boy possesses everything he needs to be a man, but it will take time and there must be growth before it is manifest what is there in essence. What is not there in essence will never manifest itself.

At regeneration, the Lord plants the essence of faith in the soul. This essence consists of the propensity to know God rightly and to trust Him with a hearty confidence. Knowledge, assent, and confidence are the components of the true faith planted in the soul, without which no one can be saved—and without which no one may partake of the Lord's Supper. However, as knowledge, assent, and confidence will be minimal in a small child, likewise also faith, hope, and love will only function very deficiently in the little ones in grace. This deficiency is not to be found in faith itself, but rather, in the believer. If the Form for the Lord's Supper would have stated, "whether he *assuredly* doth believe this faithful promise of God," then the authors of the Form would have established the measure or strength of faith as the touchstone for self-examination. They then would have set up the quintessence of faith as this touchstone, rather than its essence, but it is evident from the remainder of the Form that this was by no means their intent.

We read there:

> But this is not designed (dearly beloved brethren and sisters in the Lord), to deject the contrite hearts of the faithful, as if none might come to the supper of the Lord but those who are without sin; for we do not come to this supper to testify thereby that we are perfect and righteous in ourselves; but on the contrary, considering that we seek our life out of ourselves in Jesus Christ we acknowledge that we

lie in the midst of death; therefore, notwithstanding we feel many infirmities and miseries in ourselves, as namely, that we have not perfect faith, and that we do not give ourselves to serve God with that zeal as we are bound, but have daily to strive with the weakness of our faith and the evil lusts of our flesh; yet, since we are (by the grace of the Holy Spirit) sorry for these weaknesses, and earnestly desirous to fight against our unbelief and to live according to all the commandments of God; therefore we rest assured that no sin or infirmity which still remaineth against our will in us can hinder us from being received of God in mercy, and from being made worthy partakers of this heavenly meat and drink.

In the prayer preceding the Lord's Supper there is this petition: "That we may daily more and more with true confidence give ourselves up unto Thy Son Jesus Christ."

These quotes from the Form prove that in formulating the second touchstone for self-examination the authors in no way had in mind only those who have knowledge of the quintessence of faith, but instead, placed the emphasis entirely on the possession of the *essence* of faith. Being able to believe *assuredly* is the highest step of faith—a step not attained by all believers. Even the life of faith of God's exercised people is subject to vacillation; their faith in the faithful promises of God is far from perfect, and they by no means always believe with an assured faith!

In the words, "whether he doth believe this faithful promise of God," the measure of the believer's faith is not central, but rather, God's promise. The *promise* is faithful, that is, it is sure. God cannot and will not lie. Whatever He promises, He will do it, not for our sake, but for His great Name's sake! On whom did the Lord bequeath the promises of salvation? Only to those who are mature in grace?

As an answer to this question, we need only to read

the Beatitudes in Matthew 5. The sacraments are intended for the encouragement and strengthening of all whom the Lord pronounces blessed in Matthew 5 and elsewhere with similar pronouncements in Scripture. All the promises that we find in the Beatitudes are visibly signified and sealed in the sacraments of Baptism and the Lord's Supper. If the authors of the Form would have had the quintessence rather than the essence of faith in mind, as has been explained above, they would not have been aligned with the Author of the Beatitudes.

Rev. G. H. Kersten has used another very simple example to make clear what the difference is between the essence and the quintessence of faith. He uses the example of an acorn. An acorn contains the entire oak tree. A "tree of righteousness"[2] (a mature believer) is essentially no different than an "acorn" in grace. They both belong to the same family. They are both believers, even though the oak tree has more knowledge, assurance, and comfort of belonging to this family than does the acorn. The Lord also instituted the Lord's Supper for the growth of the acorns.

---

2. The Dutch reads: "eikebomen der gerechtigheid" (Isa. 61:3)—that is, "oak trees of righteousness."

Discussion Questions

1. What do you think must be known in order to partake of the Lord's Supper? Does your standard agree with what the Belgic Confession, the Heidelberg Catechism, and the Form for the Lord's Supper require for partaking of the Lord's Supper?

2. What is the difference between believing in God's sure promises and believing assuredly in God's promises?

3. Is the Lord's Supper only instituted for those who assuredly believe God's promises?

4. Does this assured believing belong to the essence or the quintessence of faith?

5. Why do you think some of God's children do not partake of the Lord's Supper, and others only sporadically obey the Lord's commandment of love?

Weak Faith is Also Faith

In his book *The Devout Communicant*, which has been a blessing for so many, Petrus Immens earnestly endeavored to show that not only those who possess full assurance of faith must partake of the Lord's Supper, but also those who are grieved and concerned about the fact that they lack this assurance. Consider the disciples, for instance, when the Lord Jesus instituted the Supper. Were they men who had a sanctified and saving knowledge regarding the essence of the Lord's Supper—that is, of the necessity and profit of the death of the Lord Jesus? I do not believe so. Yet to them the Lord Jesus said, "With desire I have desired to eat this passover with you" (Luke 22:16). Should we use different standards than the Lord Himself used? Would we bar from the Lord's table those whom the Lord in His great love and care has given a sign and seal of His grace to strengthen them in and for spiritual warfare? Is it not the holy calling and duty of all office-bearers—yes, of all the godly by virtue of the office of all believers—to stir up all for whom the Lord instituted His Holy Supper to partake of it in remembrance of Him?

The disciples had to learn, unlearn, and experience much before they became mature believers. Yet, Christ greatly desired to eat this meal with them—a meal His Father commanded Him to institute.

In his third treatise, Petrus Immens affirms the following: "The fact that the author of the Heidelberg Catechism in Lord's Day 7, answering the question as to what true faith is, defines it as consisting of an assured confidence, does not prove a thing [that is, that only a steadfast trust is worthy of being designated as "faith"—AE], for upon examining this definition more closely, it presupposes a refuge-taking confidence" (p. 119).

Prior to this, Immens writes (p. 72) that Scripture uses the word "faith" in a two-fold fashion, stating that its first use signifies taking refuge (Ps. 2:12, 36:8), while the second signifies a leaning, resting, and relying upon, or permitting one's self to be carried by another like a child who safely entrusts himself to his mother (Songs 8:5, Ps. 84:13).

Alexander Comrie, in his beautiful book, *The ABC of Faith*, also labored diligently to explain in detail the various designations given in Scripture to faith and the act of believing. Only the Lord knows how many people have found this very instructive book a blessing.

From what has just been stated, it is therefore evident that the act of taking refuge to the Lord is as much a mark and act of faith as is leaning and relying on Him. In Hosea 11:11, we read that the Lord's people "shall tremble as a bird out of Egypt, and as a dove out of the land of Assyria." The Lord calls this a fruit and proof of His work—of a faith that would lead to, "And I will place them in their houses, saith the LORD."

On page 119, Petrus Immens also asserts: "There were wise reasons for defining faith in that manner [as is done in Lord's Day 7] and at the time when the (Heidelberg) Catechism was composed. Popery disputes the comforting doctrine of the assurance of salvation, and these heroes of faith have therefore opposed this, demonstrating that one can be assured of one's faith."

It needs to be understood that the Roman Catholic Church teaches that every form of spiritual assurance is a form of pride. Rome teaches that since the holiest of saints is and remains only human, we must doubt our salvation until our last breath. They reason that if a believer does not doubt, he is proud. In opposition to this theology of doubt, our fathers rightly taught that true believers can most certainly be assured, and that such assurance will be present.

This assurance does not issue forth from man himself, but proceeds from Him who is faithful and mighty, and has promised that "a bruised reed shall he not break, and the smoking flax shall he not quench" (Isa. 42:3). Such assurance is the result of casting the anchor of faith (be it with trembling hands and knees) in an anchor ground outside of ourselves, provided for us by God in Christ. Indeed, He is the God-given Prophet, Priest, and King, having been sent into the world to save sinners, and who now sits at the right hand of God for the benefit of a church He purchased at a great price. It is the Spirit of Christ who gives and works such assurance in various degrees—an assurance which is of an entirely different sort than that of which the proud boast. Such assurance will not make us proud, but humble. The foundation of such assurance is to be found in the covenant of grace—in God's covenant—and thus totally outside of the believer. The sacraments communicate this truth *sacramentally*.

Rome, teaching that good works are meritorious, rejects this doctrine. Rome has no use for the doctrine of free grace of which Peter spoke so eloquently at the apostolic council: "But we believe that through the grace of the Lord Jesus Christ we shall be saved" (Acts 15:11).

The Judaizers, whose spiritual heirs are especially found in the Roman Catholic Church, shifted the foundation of the hope for salvation from Jesus and Him crucified alone by including the observance of the ceremonial law. For them, it was Jesus and Moses; for Peter, it was Jesus alone. Through the Reformation, this word "alone" was recovered. Faith alone, the Holy Scriptures alone, and grace alone were rightfully and gloriously preached in opposition to the Roman Catholic doctrine of Scripture *and* tradition, grace *and* works, and Jesus *and* Mary.

Though Roman Catholicism boasts of Christ, it has shifted the foundation of salvation from Christ to man—from the divine to the human. Her gospel is not the same as what God Himself introduced in Paradise. The gospel made mention of Christ only; nothing of man was to be found in it and nothing would be added to it. God's true servants do not wish to preach any other gospel but this. God's true children do not wish to know of any other gospel, nor can they find life in any other gospel. God's sovereign good pleasure alone gives them hope for salvation and a foundation for assurance.

May the Lord cleanse our hearts also from this legalistic, Judaistic, and Roman Catholic leaven so that we shall neither seek nor have any other anchor for our hope than the mediatorial work and the Word of the Lord Jesus Christ.

According to Hebrews 11:1, "Faith is the substance of things hoped for, the evidence of things not seen." The fact that the authors of both the Heidelberg Catechism and the Form for the Administration of the Lord's Supper have given a more extensive and seemingly more complicated description can be attributed to the errors that were prevalent at that time concerning the essence of faith.

True faith consists of assured knowledge. There is a great difference between having assured knowledge of matters that are outside of ourselves and matters that are within ourselves. For example, it is one thing to believe that the Lord Jesus is a complete Savior, and it is another thing to believe that the Lord Jesus is *my* personal Savior. The assured knowledge of the first pertains to the object of faith: the Lord Jesus Christ. The assured knowledge of the second pertains to the subject of faith: myself.

One's assured knowledge of the first can be very strong, whereas that of the second can be very weak. The godly English divine John Owen expressed this in poetic form, saying, "It is one thing to have grace; it is another thing to know that this is the case."

A child of wealthy parents is the heir of all their possessions. He is rich from the first moment of his birth. It will, however, take years before he knows that he is rich and what the extent of his wealth is. Such a child will only gradually learn it, and only then can he make use of the inheritance, doing so at the time appointed by the testators and as regulated by law.

Such is the case also in the kingdom of heaven. All who are born again are rich—unspeakably rich. Everything is theirs. It takes time and instruction, however, to discover how rich they are in Christ, who has been made unto them wisdom, and righteousness, and sanctification, and complete redemption (1 Cor. 1:30).

When Abraham first came into Canaan, the Lord revealed to him that He would give this land to him and his seed. By way of the promise, Abraham was therefore already the possessor of this land, even though there was not a square inch of Canaan that he could call his own. At that moment, he had seen only very little of the beautiful inheritance the Lord had given him. Only by traversing the entire land of Canaan—from east to west and from north to south—and by experiencing numerous incidents would Abraham learn the extent of his inheritance.

Likewise, the heirs of God and Christ, who by grace alone are partakers of all the benefits of the covenant of grace (having been testamentally bequeathed to them), must be instructed by God's Word, Spirit, and providence about the inexpressible wealth that has become their portion—entirely without any merit of theirs. These riches, as a gift of the Lord alone, will be their eternal portion because of His eternal good pleasure.

Room must be made for every new unveiling of every portion of the treasure that has become theirs in and through Christ. Otherwise, no one would value it or make use of it in a manner pleasing to God. Not all of God's children will be led as deeply into the secrets of the Lord, which, for His covenant's sake, He will reveal to His friends (Ps. 25:14).

Some believers are well acquainted with these secrets, and others are not. While the measure of the Lord's revelation to His children is contingent upon His sovereignty and wisdom, there is also a connection to what they need for the battle arena of this life. Those whom the Lord wishes to use for the benefit of others must go through deeper ways than others. In proportion to the magnitude of the battle, they will need more assurance. The Lord gives strength according to our cross, and a cross in proportion to our strength. Therefore, we surely ought not to doubt our state of grace because we do not have as much assurance as other children of God. We may—in fact, we must—strive for growth in grace. We must learn, however, that the measure of this grace is to be left to the wisdom and sovereignty of the Lord, "dividing to every man severally as he wills" (1 Cor. 12:11).

Paul wrote to the Thessalonians, "For our gospel came not unto you in word only, but also in power, and in the Holy Ghost, and in much assurance" (1 Thess. 1:5). The gospel may come to us in power and in the Holy Ghost with less assurance. This was evidently the case in Paul's days. Thus it has been and thus it will be. We may and must seek much assurance so that God will be all the more glorified by us; God, however, disposes. "Lo, all that put their trust in Him [whatever the measure of this may be], are blest indeed, and blest for aye" (Psalter 4:5). I wish to write a bit more about the assurance inherent in putting our trust in the Lord.

To understand correctly what this means, we need to know that there is assurance of faith and an assurance of sense. There can be the first without the latter. Julie von Hausmann, near the end of her life, wrote in a poem, "When I feel nothing of Thy might, Thou art accomplishing Thy purpose in my life, even during the night."[1] When Job did not see or feel anything of the Lord's help and assistance, he testified, "Though he slay me, yet will I trust in him" (Job 13:15). In Isaiah 66:2b, we read, "But to this man will I look, even to him that is poor and of a contrite spirit, and trembleth at my word." In Isaiah 57:15, the Lord speaks in similar fashion: "Thus saith the high and lofty One that inhabiteth eternity, whose name is Holy; I dwell in the high and holy place, with him also that is of a contrite and humble spirit, to revive the spirit of the humble, and to revive the heart of the contrite ones."

No one will deny that the people to whom the Lord speaks these encouraging words, giving them such comforting promises, are true believers. The Lord instituted the Holy Supper for them in order that, in His own words, He may turn His hand upon the little ones (Zech. 13:7b). Such people may and must partake of the Lord's Supper for the strengthening of their faith.

The Lord invites them to His table so that they may receive nourishment on the pathway of life. The loving invitation is in its essence a loving command. The command, "This do in remembrance of me," must be obeyed out of love for Him. Not one believer would contradict this. It is, however, a great matter to take one's place at the Table of the Covenant. There is the fear of eating and drinking

---

1. The German text reads as follows: "Wenn ich auch gar nichts fühle von Deiner Macht, Du bringst mich doch zum Ziele, auch durch die Nacht."

damnation to one's self, the fear of deceiving one's self upon self-examination, and the fear of lacking the wedding garment. All of this makes it far from simple to be obedient to the Lord's will.

Difficulties can arise when we consider the first touchstone for self-examination used in the Form for the Lord's Supper: "First, that every one consider by himself, his sins and the curse due to him for them, to the end that he may abhor and humble himself before God, considering that the wrath of God against sin is so great that (rather than it should go unpunished) He hath punished the same in His beloved Son Jesus Christ with the bitter and shameful death of the cross." This can be the case when we consider the answer to Question 81 of the Heidelberg Catechism, in which is written that the Lord's Supper is instituted for those who are truly sorrowful for their sins.[2]

For some true believers, one of the greatest problems in self-examination is found in ascertaining the truthfulness, genuineness, and quality of this loathing of self. Have I been sufficiently convicted of my guilt? Is my contrition sufficient? Am I sufficiently poor in spirit? Do I tremble sufficiently at God's Word? Have I been sufficiently humbled? Am I sufficiently contrite in spirit? Do I sufficiently mourn for my sins?

When answering these questions, we need to keep in mind that the answers do not come from others or from ourselves, but from the Lord. Weighed in the scales of God's justice, the penitence of every human and every child of God will be found wanting.

In those scales, only the Lord Jesus and what He has accomplished will be sufficient. Only when robed in the garment of Christ's righteousness can a sinner find grace

---

2. The Dutch translation of the Catechism reads: "Voor degenen, die zichzelf vanwege hun zonden mishagen"—that is, "For those who loathe themselves because of their sins."

in the holy eyes of the Lord. That is the only way to cover the filthy smudges of my sin with which I am defiled before His all-seeing eye. Whoever ventures to come before God at His table with a different "wedding garment" will experience that this greatly displeases the Lord. However, anyone who takes refuge as a penitent sinner under the robe of righteousness of Christ's mediatorial work will experience that God is merciful and that His tender mercies and lovingkindnesses have been ever of old (Ps. 25:6).

In His mercy, the Lord has declared in His Word (which alone has the final word concerning all that pertains to the kingdom of God) that "He…shall save the souls of the needy" (Ps. 72:13). The word "needy" is the translation of a Hebrew word that means "to be in want." Thus, to be needy means to lack something we cannot be without. This perception of want makes us needy; the fact that we are in want causes us to mourn. However, we cannot produce what we lack. We cannot acquire it ourselves. What misery! What poverty!

Anyone who considers his own knowledge of his misery to be sufficient (upon examining himself regarding the first thing that must be known to live, attend the Lord's table, and die in comfort), will receive a failing mark from the Lord. Whoever gives himself a passing mark is a proud person. To such Psalm 138:6 applies: "But the proud he knoweth afar off."

That is the spiritual disposition of the infamous Pharisee who gave himself nothing but passing grades. The publican gave himself nothing but failing grades for all aspects of his self-examination, and yet, he went home justified—that is, God declared him just. How the mercy of God shines forth in this testimony regarding the publican! What divine justice shines forth in God's testimony regarding the Pharisee! He who condemns himself will not be condemned, but he who justifies himself will be condemned indeed. That is the meaning of this well-known parable. He who justifies himself cannot and will not be justified by God, for every human being comes short in all things—even in his penitence. When is our penitence sufficient in the scales of God's mercy? That will not be determined by the quantity of tears we shed, the measure of contrition about the sins we have committed, or the measure of sorrow to be found in our hearts. No, God has given a different touchstone—even though the penitence that is acceptable in God's sight will not be without the things just mentioned. What is this touchstone?

We read in Ezekiel 36:31, "Then shall ye remember your own evil ways, and your doings that were not good, and shall lothe yourselves in your own sight for your iniquities and for your abominations." This loathing of self is the criterion that counts. If that is lacking, the most important element in our penitence will be lacking. No, it does not say that those mentioned in Ezekiel 36:31 loathe themselves *sufficiently*. A fallen human being can never loathe himself sufficiently. For a sinner (which God's child remains until his last breath) there is not a single aspect of his life that is acceptable, and would render him righteous before God.

What was it that brought Luther to despair in his striving to render himself pleasing and acceptable before God? He was never sufficiently humbled, never sufficiently sorrowful, never sufficiently contrite, never sufficiently holy. In spite of his most vehement efforts to accomplish this, it was always insufficient!

What was it that delivered Luther from this prison in which he dwelt for such a long time? His spiritual eyes were opened to see Him whose suffering and obedience were sufficient. The righteousness of Christ, revealed and offered in the gospel as a garment for the naked and righteousness for the unrighteous, was sufficient to cover

eternally all sin and failure. This divine revelation caused
Luther to look away from himself and to seek refuge as a
wretched sinner by faith in the righteousness of Christ.
This opened the gateway to heaven for him. After so many
years of being locked up in the prison of legalism, Luther
jubilated, "I received all that was His, and He took all that
was mine!" What a deliverance, and how liberating! Did
this mean that Luther had permanently been delivered
from legalism? No, for until his death he had to wrestle
with the pope in his heart. The twitches of the old man still
caused him much grief. However, even though Satan and
self did everything in their power to draw him away and to
subject him again to legal bondage, they did not fully succeed. The Lord Himself saw to this and took care of this.
What a faithful Savior He is!

Where does the loathing of one's self mentioned in
Ezekiel 36:31 come from? From man himself? Never! We
are too proud for this. No, that is the work of Him who
said, "They shall lothe themselves for the evils which they
have committed in all their abominations" (Ezek. 6:9);
"Not for your sakes do I this, saith the Lord GOD, be it
known unto you: be ashamed and confounded for your
own ways, O house of Israel" (Ezek. 36:32).

Shame for sin, loathing of self, and sorrow and contrition are the scriptural marks of a penitent sinner of whom
the Lord says in Psalm 138:6, "Though the LORD be high,
yet hath he respect unto the lowly."

Whenever these matters are present in some measure,
they are to be viewed as the fruits of the Spirit—though
they will always seem insufficient. Though we should always seek to attain a greater measure of these things, yet
this regretful insufficiency in our penitence will not prevent
God from receiving us graciously and viewing us as worthy
guests at His table in order to render us fit to receive the
heavenly food and drink.

When the knowledge of our misery is such that it has brought us as a beggar at the throne of grace, confessing that we are worthy to be cast away forever and motivating us to seek our purification and salvation outside of ourselves in Christ Jesus, this will be sufficient in God's judgment to show us mercy for Christ's sake.

The sufficiency of all this flows from the fact that He acknowledges this as His own work—a work that is necessary and beneficial to salvation and the glorification of His Name. In this way, His Name will eternally receive all honor by those whom He has loved with an everlasting love, and has graciously chosen and prepared to show forth His praises. Of Him, through Him, and unto Him are all things!

But how can being poor and contrite in spirit, trembling at God's Word, and having the broken heart we read of in the Form for the Lord's Supper be compatible with the second touchstone set forth in the Heidelberg Catechism (Q & A 81)? Do we not read there "...and yet trust that these are forgiven them for the sake of Christ; and that their remaining infirmities are covered by His passion and death"? Does the latter not exclude the former? Can these two matters go together? How can the mark of having a humble spirit, being contrite, and being sorry for our sin (a mark of those whom God will bless) be compatible with what the authors of the Form for the Lord's Supper have set forth in their second touchstone? "That every one examine his own heart whether he doth believe this faithful promise of God that all his sins are forgiven him only for the sake of the passion and death of Jesus Christ, and that the perfect righteousness of Christ is imputed and freely given him as his own, yea, so perfectly, as if he had satisfied in his own person for all his sins and fulfilled all righteousness."

As I already stated, we must view this formulation against the background of the battle against the Roman

Catholic theology of doubt. Furthermore, we must keep in mind that when the Bible, the confessions, and the forms speak of assurance in connection with baptism and the Lord's Supper, a distinction needs to be made between the assurance of *faith* and the assurance of *sense*. Before I could discuss this distinction in more detail, I wanted to avoid misunderstandings. In the next chapter, I will extend a helping hand to arrive at a proper understanding regarding this distinction.

Discussion Questions

1. Why have the authors of the Heidelberg Catechism and the Form for the Lord's Supper, in responding to the question for whom the Lord's Supper has been instituted, posited that a certain measure of confidence is a prerequisite?

2. Is the Roman Catholic Church correct in her claim that to have an assured confidence is pride and that the fostering of doubt is humility?

3. What is meant by the expression "the steps of grace"?

4. On the basis of Scripture, can you identify any of these steps?

5. Why is it that not all who are in the same state of grace arrive at the same level of grace?

6. How can partaking of the Lord's Supper be subservient to growth in grace?

The Assurance of Faith and the Assurance of Sense

Alexander Comrie, among others, has written about the difference between the assurance of faith and the assurance of sense. In Comrie's exposition of the Heidelberg Catechism, we read the following:

> We must always make a distinction between the assurance of faith and the assurance of sense. Failure to make this distinction will bring about extraordinary darkness and confusion in the minds of many, confusing two matters that need to be clearly distinguished from one another.
>
> The assurance of faith rests solely on God's truth, bequeathed upon us in the divine promise, by which we, trusting the Word of the promising God, appropriate the promise in such a fashion that we consider the matter promised to be ours. With confidence we view it as such prior to the actual possession of this matter—albeit that thousands of difficulties along with the appearance of impossibility militate against this.
>
> Unless I am seriously mistaken, I believe this to be the meaning of Paul's words in Romans 4:18–21, "Who against hope believed in hope, that he might become the father of many nations, according to that which was spoken, So shall thy seed be. And being not weak in faith, he considered not his own body now dead, when he was about an hundred

years old, neither yet the deadness of Sara's womb:
He staggered not at the promise of God through
unbelief; but was strong in faith, giving glory to
God; and being fully persuaded that, what he had
promised, he was able also to perform"—i.e., he did
not stumble in spite of all the impossibilities that
militated against its fulfillment and which hindered
him in embracing the promise.

Thus you see that, as an assured confidence belongs to the very nature of faith itself, the activity of
faith is neither focused on the likely fulfillment of the
promise, nor on the actual possession of the matter
promised, but rather, it rests solely upon the Word of
the God who cannot lie—the God who has faithfulness as the girdle of His reins (Isa. 11:5) and whose
truth is a buckler and shield (Ps. 91:4). Therefore, all
the impossibilities which present themselves will not
prevent the fulfillment of the promise, for faith does
not reason with flesh and blood. Rather, even in darkness, when there is not a ray of hope, it will trust in
the Name of the LORD and lean upon its God.

When we trust in God's Word *without seeing,
possessing, or feeling,* then we will have rest, even in
the swelling of Jordan (Jer. 12:5)—yes, even if the
earth were to be removed and all the mountains
of possibilities be carried into the midst of the sea
(Ps. 46:2). This assured confidence of faith causes
one to dwell, so to speak, in a stronghold. All the
Reformers viewed this assured confidence, anchored
in the promise, as belonging to the essence rather
than the quintessence of faith—even though it is
often under assault due to the weakness of the flesh
and the manifold assaults of unbelief against which
we must do battle.

It testifies of ignorance to insist that they understood an assured confidence to mean that he who
has been gifted with true faith necessarily has the
assurance of *sense* that he is a partaker of Christ and
all His benefits. There is nothing in the Catechism

that would give us such a notion. Everything has been formulated in such a way that we would understand that the authors had the assurance of *faith* in mind, whereby we are assured that not only to others but also to us the forgiveness of sins and eternal life have been granted.

The assurance of sense consists of a joyous emotion that arises in the heart from an inner conviction wrought in the heart by the Holy Spirit that we truly have and enjoy all that is promised. This is the awareness of the joy of God's salvation by virtue of the Spirit witnessing with our spirit, causing us to behold, to our joy, what has been given to us by God. Though this is delightful for the soul, this is neither enjoyed by all nor is it enjoyed at all times. Rather, it is very often assaulted—assaulted so much by Satan and unbelief that one is ready to die (Ps. 88:15). All the while, however, the assurance of faith, in the absence of the assurance of sense, can be very strong, as can be seen in Psalm 88 and elsewhere. It would be profitable to read our great Calvin (*Institutes*, 3.2.17) whose personal words we would share with you if it were not so lengthy and would hold us up too much. (Utrecht, the Netherlands: De Banier, 1941, p. 491.)

A simple example from Scripture may clarify Comrie's writing. When Abraham was seventy-five years old, the Lord promised him a son. As long as Isaac was not born, Abraham lacked the assurance of *sense* in regard to this matter; that is, the tangible fulfillment of God's promise.

The fulfillment of this promise came about when he held Isaac in his arms. It was the assurance of *faith* (which at times was stronger than at other times, as was evident from Abraham's failures) that gave strength to Abraham and Sarah who judged "him faithful who had promised" (Heb. 11:11).

When the authors of the Heidelberg Catechism say in Question 81 that the Lord's Supper has been instituted for all who trust that their sins "are forgiven them for the sake of Christ; and that their remaining infirmities are covered by His passion and death," they do not have the assurance of *sense* in mind (i.e., feeling that their sins are forgiven them), but rather, the assurance of *faith* which focuses on God's Word. "If we confess our sins, he is faithful and just to forgive us our sins, and to cleanse us from all unrighteousness" (1 John 1:9). The Lord spoke, "When I see the blood, I will pass over you" (Ex. 12:13). All who take refuge with their sins and misery in the blood of Christ, which "speaks better things than the blood of Abel" and was typified by the blood of the Paschal Lamb, may build their hope on this sure promise. The foundation of that hope does not rest on a *sense* of this passing over (albeit that this will be very comforting and delightful for the soul to experience this), but rather in God's *promise* that He will pass over.

This trust in God's *promises* needs to be nourished by partaking of the Lord's Supper. Partaking at the table counters the fears and concerns that trouble the anxious heart and cause it to cry out, "Hath God forgotten to be gracious? hath he in anger shut up his tender mercies?" (Ps. 77:9). Only the Lord is able to remove such anxiety by working and strengthening faith and conviction in His promises until their fulfillment is accomplished. Hearing His Word and the use of the sacraments are the means which the Lord uses to accomplish this. Through the administration of the sacraments, the Lord assures us that He is gracious and faithful, and it pleases Him to increase the assurance of *faith* in both His grace and faithfulness through them. Occasionally He permits someone to enjoy the assurance of *sense* at the same time. This, however, is an added gift.

It cannot possibly be true that the authors of the Form for the Lord's Supper assert in the second touchstone for self-examination that we must possess the assurance of *sense* in order to be worthy partakers of this Supper. It is of the utmost importance that a sharp distinction be maintained between the assurance of faith and that of sense. Ignorance regarding this matter has brought many people into great confusion—yes, even to the verge and depths of despair.

Comrie is not the only one who has pointed out the distinction between the assurance of faith and that of sense. Petrus Immens, a forefather loved because of his piety and sanctified wisdom, gave much attention to this matter in his book, *The Devout Communicant*. Immens writes,

There is more than one kind of assurance.

a. There is an objective assurance, which may be defined as a full persuasion and reliance with respect to all that God has revealed in His Word regarding Himself, of the Lord Jesus, and of the whole plan of salvation. The apostle John speaks of this as receiving the testimony of God, whereby we set to our seal that God is true. This kind of assurance, in principal, has respect to God as its object, and is necessarily included in assurance. But,

b. There is also an assurance which respects the person that believes; for it is one thing to know and believe that there is a God and a Savior, and another to be persuaded that He is my God, and my Savior. This subjective assurance is again to be considered as being of two kinds:

1. The one may be styled ordinary and is produced in the soul on this wise. When the believer looks into the Word of God and becomes aware of what is declared with respect to the heirs of salvation, to wit, that they have fled for refuge to lay hold on the hope set before them; that they hunger and thirst after the righteousness of Christ; that God takes away their stony heart and gives them a heart of flesh; that they desire

to love God as their strength; and desire to follow after holiness, without which no man can see the Lord; and after examining his heart on all these points, the result, in a lesser or greater degree, will be that he concludes that he is an heir of salvation. [From the context and that which follows, it is evident that he is presently discussing the assurance of *faith*, and not that of *sense*—Author's note].

2. The other may be called extraordinary, which is experienced when God seals faith and love in their heart [that is, the assurance of *sense*—AE], and views them with favor and delight.

Consider the following similitude, in order to rightly comprehend the distinction between ordinary and extraordinary assurance. A child, absent from his father for some time, will run to meet him as soon as he sees his father's face. If you ask this child why he does this, he will readily reply, because I sincerely love my father. When the father sees his child coming, he does not ignore his child, but lovingly embraces his child and takes him or her up in his arms. The natural conclusion is that the child not only can say I love my father, but that my father also loves me. So to exercise love, and to be embraced in love are two distinct things. Although a soul may do the former for many years, the latter is only experienced by a believer on particular occasions; and in some instances the Lord does not privilege His people to experience this until their deathbed.

It is one thing to surrender ourselves, and another to have a sense of acceptance. The first can be exercised frequently for years, such as by a humble and believing partaking of the Lord's Supper, being obedient to the Lord's loving command. The latter, however, can be absent for years and will not always be experienced by those who, at times, were privileged to experience a sensible affirmation of the Lord's favor. The prayer preceding the administration and partaking of the Lord's Supper (in the Form for the Lord's Supper) contains the following petition: "Oh most merciful God and Father, we beseech Thee that…we may daily more and more with true confidence give ourselves up unto Thy Son Jesus Christ." This surrender in true confidence is therefore not yet what it ought to be, for there is still so much doubt, and the act of surrender itself is deficient. To our grief, the three graces—faith, hope, and love—are not yet what they ought to be, and therefore, "Oh God, for Christ's sake, who did suffer and does intercede for transgressors, grant that we may more and more—and thus with more and more genuine confidence—give ourselves up to Thy Son Jesus Christ." Such surrender is a matter of *faith*, building on nothing else than God's Word. Having an affirmation of the Lord's favor is a matter of *sense*.

Immens speaks likewise:

> Be not too much set upon having your comfort and joy derived from a feeling sense of divine grace and of the operations of the Holy Spirit. If it pleases the Lord to grant you those sensible evidences of His love, be thankful; highly prize and carefully preserve them, but if you have not these experiences, consider that now you are not so much called to feel as to believe. The former is transitory but the latter remains when feelings cease. The one produces a tender, steadfast walk, but the other renders it wavering and unsteady. As long as a person has a feeling of the love of God, he conceives that hills and mountains must fall before him, and says, "I shall never be moved," but if he loses this feeling sense, the least unfavorable circumstance alarms him, and he is ready to give up all for lost. But faith continues though midnight darkness rest upon us. By believing, we keep a fast hold of the Word and

promises, and thus temptations of every kind lose much of their power.

How frequently, in those who have some felt sense of God's grace and love, do doubts vanish and inward assaults silence, and they will say, "Oh, how I wish that the Lord's Supper would be administered now! I would have freedom to partake." But when the Lord's Supper is administered later, and such sensible manifestations are lacking, they frequently lose the courage to participate. This occurs because we live too much by feelings and too little by the Word of God—too much by the moment and not by the immutability of God's grace and faithfulness. To cure us of that tendency, Christ instituted the Lord's Supper. He does not change, even though we change a thousand times—even though our feelings sometimes change several times a day. Especially when it is night within and without, how difficult it is to put our hope exclusively in God's faithfulness!

Immens states the following:

> You may perhaps say, "This would indeed be the case, were I to continue in that comfortable frame in which I found myself at the table, but it often happens that I have no sooner left it than I lose that comfortable and delightful experience of the love of God shed abroad in my heart, and hence my soul is again enveloped in darkness." This may indeed be the case with you, for God designs by this to teach you not to walk by sight but by faith.

May the Lord grant that what Comrie, Immens, and I have written will help you to understand that the foremost purpose of the Lord's Supper is to strengthen our faith and not our feelings. If the latter is also experienced, it will be sweet indeed.

It is understandable that we desire to have a measure of the assurance of sense prior to partaking of the Lord's Supper. The Lord often grants this to His children, especially prior to their first Communion. He knows how great the strife can be at times for His children before they have the courage to partake for the first time, and since they need something extra before taking this step, the Lord will frequently give it to them.

This does not mean, however, that the Lord will always do this at everyone's first time or at every Lord's Supper. At times, we give something extra to our children simply because they need it. Sometimes adults get something extra under special circumstances. But then, when we try to make these "extras" the norm, things will go awry. When our children are growing up but in some areas insist on being treated as infants (sometimes adults act this way also!), as parents we may not yield to this. In order to facilitate growth toward adulthood, we may withhold from our children something we would not have withheld from them earlier. This is an essential component of proper training, for it will promote their growth and maturity. To simply yield to childish wishes is convenient for us as parents, but may not be subservient to the well-being of our children.

This is not how the Lord trains His children. In weakness, we frequently yield to our children when they persist in asking for something they do not really need, but the Lord will not do this. If we truly need it and if He deems it desirable and profitable, He will give the assurance of sense prior to the Lord's Supper. Experience confirms this. However, it is incorrect to make it normative that we *must* have the assurance of sense prior to the first, or to any, partaking of the Lord's Supper. The purpose of the Lord's Supper is to *be* strengthened during and following its use. We must not reverse the order that God has established. We must first believe, and then we shall feel and see. When a doctor prescribes something that will strengthen a weak person, such means must be used immediately. Who would not condemn the weak patient who responded to the doctor's prescription by saying, "I'll wait to use what the doctor has prescribed for me until I am stronger"? This also applies to the partaking of the Lord's Supper which the Lord has prescribed for the strengthening of the faith of the believer. The Lord requires child-like obedience to His command of love so that *His* good pleasure may be accomplished. Child-like bickering that aims to accomplish *our* good pleasure is something that displeases the Lord. He accomplishes His will by His Word, as well as by the way in which He leads us. He thus cures us from our bickering through His Word and providence, doing so as a gracious, longsuffering, merciful, and tender Savior.

This process of unlearning and learning progresses slowly. In spite of all opposition and resistance from flesh and blood, however, the Lord will not cease to lead His own to spiritual maturity. Also in the Lord's Supper, He calls for child-like obedience and unconditional surrender, in order for His people to experience that He does indeed look upon those who are poor and of a contrite spirit, and who tremble at His Word (Isa. 66:2). It pleases Him to do so by way of the administration of the Lord's Supper.

Again, he who considers his conformity to any component of the form's three Scriptural touchstones for self-examination to be sufficient knows and experiences his misery insufficiently. God will give such a person a failing mark. He or she is still proud—or has again become proud. The humble person will give himself a failing mark for everything. "Jehovah looketh from on high with kindly eye upon the lowly, but knoweth those from far who hide, in sinful pride, their ways unholy" (Psalter 429:3).

He who knows his sins and misery sufficiently, according to the benchmark of God's *mercy*, gives himself a failing mark for every component of the test set before us in the form. In view of the benchmark of God's justice, only the mediatorial work of Christ is sufficient, and he who is utterly destitute and takes refuge to nothing else but Christ's righteousness will experience that the Lord is plenteous in mercy (Ps. 86:5).

Loathing ourselves, humbly supplicating for mercy for Christ's sake, seeking our purification and salvation outside of ourselves, and sincerely desiring and endeavoring to live according to God's will are the criteria which God establishes in His Word as prerequisites for a worthy eating and drinking of His Supper. When we loathe ourselves for an insufficient sense of our guilt; for insufficient sorrow over sin; for insufficiently striving against sin; for insufficient faith in God, Christ, and God's promises; for insufficient zeal to serve God privately and publicly, in the home and beyond—this delights the Lord. This is His work according to the judgment of God's mercy as revealed in His Word. It is to make people who in and of themselves are "rich, and increased with goods, and have need of nothing," to become such people who know that they are "wretched, and miserable, and poor, and blind, and naked" (Rev. 3:17). He makes poor in order to make rich—but then not rich in ourselves, but rich in Christ and rich in God. With all the benefits of redemption merited by Him, Christ stands at the door and petitions, "Behold, I stand at the door, and knock: if any man hear my voice, and open the door, I will come in to him, and will sup with him, and he with me" (Rev. 3:20).

God wants to fill empty vessels, and He will fill "the hungry with good things" (Luke 1:53). "The poor man's cause He will maintain, the needy He will bless" (Psalter 193:3). His will is that on His command the net be cast on the side of the boat where He said a catch would be, and we do so, hoping against hope in His unfailing Word. Even though you feel that you have not "caught" anything yet, you still must cast out the net, until He will also be gracious to you.

Not our will, but God's will must be the benchmark for our conduct. Old, blind Isaac, when blessing his sons, depended on his feelings and acted accordingly, and made a serious mistake. He should have inquired at the mouth of the Lord with his doubts. Had he done so, the Lord would surely have informed him that he was on the verge of doing something that would be entirely wrong. Isaac failed to do this, however, and great confusion, untold misery, and many years of grief came about from his one act, but I will be the last one to cast a stone at erring Isaac. Regrettably, I have erred more frequently than he. Therefore, let it be our prayer,

Direct my footsteps in Thy word,
From sin's dominion save my soul,
From man's oppression set me free,
That I may yield to Thy control.

— Psalter 337:3

Discussion Questions

1. What is the difference between the assurance of faith and the assurance of sense?

2. Can there be assurance of faith without assurance of sense?

3. Must someone possess the assurance of sense prior to partaking of the Lord's Supper?

4. Which kind of assurance is it that the Lord particularly desires to strengthen by means of partaking of the Lord's Supper, and why?

5. According to the benchmark of God's mercy, when is the knowledge of misery, redemption, and gratitude sufficient for Him to deem us a worthy guest at His table?

—5—

Touchstones for Self-Examination

In the previous chapters, we addressed the touchstones for self-examination given in the Form for the Lord's Supper. Now we wish to consider them in greater detail.

There is no doubt that they who are poor and contrite in spirit and who tremble at God's Word, of whom the Lord says that He will look favorably to them (Isa. 66:2), are invited by Him to partake of the Lord's Supper. Since the fulfillment of these promises is signified and sealed in the Lord's Supper, then they to whom these promises are made for their instruction, encouragement, and comfort, clearly may and must partake of the Lord's Supper, so that their trust in God's grace and faithfulness may be strengthened.

But when we read in the Form's second touchstone for self-examination that the Lord deems those who "believe this faithful promise of God that all his sins are forgiven him only for the sake of the passion and death of Jesus Christ, and that the perfect righteousness of Christ is imputed and freely given him as his own, yea, so perfectly, as if he had satisfied in his own person for all his sins and fulfilled all righteousness" to be worthy guests at the table of His Son, are the authors of the Form establishing a different standard? Is being poor and contrite in spirit and trembling at God's Word compatible with believing the promise that my sins are forgiven me and that Christ's righteousness is mine? Are these contradictory? Does the one not preclude the other?

In contradistinction to the Roman Catholic error of redemption through Christ *plus* one's own works, the authors
of the Form wanted to establish very clearly that if anyone
trusts for redemption in anything other than Christ, even if
it were but a sigh and a tear, he would invoke the displeasure of God. In doing so, he would be guilty of establishing
a foundation other than what God has established in the
Person and work of His Son Jesus Christ. There is only one
basis on which God can and will be gracious, and that is the
active and passive obedience of Christ. This is the sole and
exclusive foundation for God's faithful promises. Nothing
can or needs to be added to Christ's work in order to be a
partaker of God's blessings. The only basis on which God
will deal graciously with us is the imputation of Christ's active and passive obedience, doing so solely because of His
sovereign good pleasure.

In the second touchstone, the authors of the Form
compel us to examine whether we believe God's faithful
and gracious promises to be grounded in nothing other
than Christ's work; whether we expect salvation from
nothing other than God's imputation of the work of Christ
who has suffered and prayed for transgressors. The question is whether we expect our salvation from grace alone,
or whether we expect it from our own performance, be it
fully or partially? Do we expect salvation on the basis of
our humbling of ourselves before God? Or is the hope of
our salvation grounded in God's faithful promises to the
poor, to the contrite in spirit, and to them who tremble
at His Word, and thus founded on the active and passive
obedience of Christ? To be poor and contrite in spirit; to
be sincerely sorrowful that we lie in the midst of death; to
tremble at God's Word when considering how we are worthy of condemnation; to seek our purification and salvation
outside of ourselves in Christ Jesus; to desire henceforth to
show true gratitude toward the Lord God with my whole

life and to walk uprightly before God's countenance; to be sincerely inclined henceforth to live in true love and harmony with my neighbor—all are fruits and evidences of regeneration, proceeding from God's imputation of Christ's active and passive obedience to His own. The language of Colossians 2:13 is very clear regarding this matter: "And you, being dead in your sins and the uncircumcision of your flesh, hath he quickened together with him, having forgiven you all trespasses."

What our fathers establish to be a touchstone for self-examination in the Form for the Lord's Supper in no wise contradicts what the Lord teaches in His Word. They formulated it as such because the Roman Catholic teaching compelled them to do so. The notion of building our salvation on something of ourselves may not be entertained. On the contrary! There is only one ground for the anchor of our hope: Jesus Christ and Him crucified. There is only one righteousness that saves from death: the righteousness of Jesus Christ.

They who are truly poor and contrite of spirit and who tremble at God's Word cannot and will not hear of any other foundation for their hope than Jesus Christ and Him crucified. They have been stripped of everything outside of Christ. In this way, and by the drawing power of the Holy Spirit through the gospel, they will be drawn, for the first time or afresh, to take refuge in the person and blood of Christ. They are not willing to trust in anything of themselves.

It grieves them that they still find so much unbelief, doubt, and legalism within themselves. They groan that the Lord would deliver them from it. They are the truly poor who are of a contrite spirit and who tremble at God's Word, counting all things but loss for the excellency of the knowledge of Christ Jesus that they may win Christ, and be found in Him, not having their own righteousness but His

(Phil. 3:8–9). They have not yet attained this excellency, but they follow after it (Phil. 3:12). Since they find so much deficiency in themselves (Rom. 7), they remain poor and contrite in spirit and continue to tremble at God's Word.

These are the people the Lord deems worthy partakers at the table of His Son Jesus Christ. God's Word teaches this in many places, and our fathers did not teach and instruct otherwise in the Form for the Lord's Supper. When we read into their words something other than they intended to say, it is not their fault but ours that they are misunderstood. Our ignorance causes us to err. May the Lord pardon our ignorance for Christ's sake and teach us true wisdom by His Spirit, so that all confusion may vanish—also in regard to the question for whom the Lord's Supper has been instituted.

They who put their trust in God's Word deal wisely, however much our flesh and blood may militate against this. God's Word says of the sacraments that they have been instituted to instruct, encourage, and comfort those who are declared blessed in the Beatitudes. Though they lack the fulfillment of what they miss, lack everything for which their hearts yearn, and do not fully possess what their hearts long for, they already possess these things *in the promise!* This means that in God's time they will surely become partakers of all that has been promised by the appropriating ministry of the Holy Spirit. Word and sacrament exhort us to believe this divine truth and to trust that God, by virtue of His grace and faithfulness, will fulfill His promises by granting them what they lack. God will hear and help those who neither can nor do cease to lift up their hearts to Him until He also will be gracious to them. "Hath he said, and shall he not do it?" (Num. 23:19). To whoever knocks, it *shall* be opened. According to the word of Christ, the elect (Luke 18:17) will surely be heard and helped!

The congregation of the Lord sings, "The heavens

praise, O Lord, Thy wonders day and night; Thy saints on earth extol Thy faithfulness and might" (Psalter 422:3). The Lord displays this faithfulness in all His works, but He does so in a very special manner when the Lord's Supper is administered. The words of Psalter 252:4, "But mighty is the Lord our God, above the raging sea. Thy testimonies, Lord, in faithfulness excel," are visibly confirmed when we may behold the manifestation of the Lord's eternal and sovereign good pleasure in the congregation, as well as the loveliness of His blessed service.

Blessed are they who observe all this and whose souls may thereby be strengthened to hope in the Lord and His salvation. To them who with all their sins and wretchedness cannot cease to turn unto Him for mercy, the promises of God's mercy are visibly set before them for their encouragement. God has eternally purposed that, by His Word and Spirit, they should learn to take refuge to Him for their redemption, and that in doing so they should experience His salvation. They are invited to feed on the promises of God, made visible and tangible in the broken bread and poured out wine, so that by partaking they may be strengthened in their souls to exercise faith in the fulfillment of God's promises, which are "yea and amen" in Christ (2 Cor. 1:20).

In the invitation to partake of the Lord's Supper, they are told, "Fear not; only believe" (Mark 8:50). By giving them the bread and the cup, the Lord says to them, "Be not faithless, but believing" (John 20:27). He who is meek and lowly of heart calls out to those who are troubled because of their sins (whatever the measure thereof may be), "Come unto me, all ye that labour and are heavy laden, and I will give you rest" (Matt. 11:28). The Lord says, "Come as you are, even if you cannot come as you ought to, or as you would desire—and even though you would like to be more deeply humbled and concerned." Do not allow this deficiency over which you mourn to prevent you from going to Him who so lovingly and sincerely invites you to come to Him. On the contrary! Let it drive you out to Him who said, "Him that cometh to me, I will in no wise cast out" (John 6:37b).

If you come in this fashion, you will not eat and drink judgment to yourself. It is a good thing to be fearful of this. It testifies of your knowledge of God and self, and of your humility. However, if you were to wait to draw near to the Lord at His table until you are free from fear of eating and drinking judgment to yourself, you would act contrary to the Lord's objective with His Supper. Granted, there are times when, in a special way, the Lord uses His Word, applied by the Spirit, to remove this fear of eating and drinking judgment to one's self. That is sweet indeed, but He does not always do this. He instituted the Lord's Supper so that, by eating His body and drinking His blood, you would gradually be delivered from fear!

At times, the Lord fulfills the promise of giving rest to all who labor and are heavy laden when we partake of the Lord's Supper, and sometimes He does so afterward. If, on your first and subsequent participation in the Lord's Supper, you do not experience this rest while eating the bread and drinking the wine (that is, a felt encouragement and comfort for which the heart yearns so much), do not immediately conclude that you have eaten and drunk damnation to yourself—that it was not good in the Lord's eyes that you partook of the Lord's Supper—but bring your circumstances before the Lord in prayer. Examine yourself before His countenance as to what your motives were in partaking of the Lord's Supper, and ask Him to shed light upon it.

It is pleasing to the Lord when for such a blessing we turn to Him alone who is the Fountain of all comfort and light. According to His unsearchable wisdom and sovereignty, He determines the moment when, according to His pleasure, He will reveal to us personally that it was and is pleasing to Him that we unconditionally surrendered ourselves to Him for salvation.

I personally had partaken of the Lord's Supper several times before I received the sense of assurance that my partaking was pleasing in God's sight. Thereafter I have frequently shown forth the death of the Lord without this assurance of sense, even though at times my assurance of faith in God's faithfulness, as revealed in His Word and signified and sealed in the sacraments, was strengthened.

I once administered the Lord's Supper in a congregation that did not have its own pastor. As I partook of and administered the Lord's Supper, experientially I missed that for which I so much yearned at His table—both for myself and others. When I returned to the place where I was lodging, I sought the Lord's face about this matter, and while on my knees, something happened that I have never been able to forget. Even during the darkest period of my life (my depression), the memory of what I experienced at that time shed light on my path. As I was exercised with what had happened during the celebration of the Lord's Supper, these words were brought to my attention: "Blest be the Lord for evermore, whose promise stands from days of yore. His word is faithful now as then; blest be His Name. Amen, Amen!" (Psalm 89:52—Psalter 243:15).

My amazement about the fitting instruction given me upon my prayer rendered me speechless for a few moments. What goodness, grace, love, and faithfulness! Not at the Lord 's Table, but in this guestroom, I experienced, "With the abundance of Thy house we shall be satisfied, From rivers of unfailing joy our thirst shall be supplied" (Psalter 94:3).

Therefore, "Your heart shall live, ye saints that seek the Lord; He helps the needy and regards their cries, those in distress the Lord will not despise" (Psalter 187:3).

Discussion Questions

1. How is being poor and of a contrite spirit compatible with being assured of the forgiveness of our sins?

2. Does the first touchstone for self-examination in the Form for the Lord's Supper focus on the measure of the knowledge of our misery?

3. Does the second touchstone for self-examination demand something that few saints possess?

4. Does the third touchstone for self-examination demand a great measure of holiness, or is the focus on sincerity?

5. Who eat and drink judgment unto themselves, and who do not?

6. Are God's children capable of eating and drinking judgment to themselves?

7. Is the unworthy partaking of the Lord's Supper an unpardonable sin?

Simplicity: The Distinguishing Mark of True Grace

One Saturday evening, a young man knocked on my door. The Lord's Supper was to be administered the next day. The previous Lord's Day I had preached a preparatory sermon entitled "The Pathway of God's Church," based on Ruth 1:19a: "So they two went...." Naomi and Ruth were both on a journey to Bethlehem, the House of Bread, so that, as unworthy and yet hungry sinners, they might receive bread out of the hand of the Lord. At this point, Naomi, an exercised child of the Lord, and Ruth were both on Israelite territory—Naomi as a native of Israel, and Ruth as a foreigner. Ruth had been wrought on by God's grace before the border between Moab and Israel; she had been tested by God's providence at this border and God's power had led her across it.

This young man had been greatly touched by what he had heard that morning. It was only recently that significant changes had occurred in his life. Those observing this were hopeful that the Lord had begun a good work in him. The young man told me that there was a great similarity between what had occurred in Ruth's life and what had transpired in his own life. He was a professing member of the congregation, but had never partaken of the Lord's Supper.

During the week of preparation, he earnestly examined

himself before God as to whether he was invited by the Lord to join His people in showing forth His death. He experienced much strife. The desire was there, but he lacked freedom. Though a great change had taken place in his life, he questioned whether this was the Lord's work or his own doing. Was he merely presuming something, or was it in truth? He could not resolve it. As he was wrestling for light from heaven, begging at the Lord's throne for an answer from Him who searches the heart, a portion of God's Word was impressed on him that filled him with great amazement: "I have loved thee with an everlasting love; therefore with lovingkindness have I drawn thee" (Jer. 31:3).

The young man told me that, for a few moments, he was speechless on his knees. It was so remarkable that it completely overwhelmed him. How could it be that the Lord looked on a "dead dog" as he was (2 Sam. 9:8), and that He loved such a wretch with an everlasting love? However, shortly thereafter he began to reason with himself; it could not really be true that the Lord loved him and would love him forever. What prompted him to doubt like this?

I relate this story because I hope that it may yield instruction either to prevent or relieve the anxiety caused by comparing yourself to others.

This young man told me—asking me whether he was deceiving himself in this—that he had said this to the Lord: "Lord, I dare not believe that Thou hast, dost, and wilt love me, and that what has transpired in my life is the result of Thy drawing love, for I have not experienced the great fear and anxiety of which I have both heard and read in regard to the experience of Thy children."

What happened at that point? The same words from Jeremiah 31:3 were impressed on him anew, and this time his attention was specifically drawn to the last part of this text: "Therefore with lovingkindness have I drawn thee."

The young man said to me, "It was as if the Lord said

to me that I should not suspect my experiences simply because they were not accompanied with great fear and intense anxiety. On the contrary! The manner in which the renewal of my life had taken place was in harmony with God's own Word—even with the manner in which God's child and servant, Jeremiah, had been led. Drawn with lovingkindness! What a wonder! I truly did not deserve this!"

You will perhaps be able to understand who the teacher and the pupil were when the young man told me this! He was not the only one who was amazed. However, there was more. During the preceding days, this young man had spent his time reading the beautiful book of Petrus Immens, *The Devout Communicant.*

To his amazement and joy, he read in the fourth chapter, among other things, "Let such learn to attend with care to the ways of God in dispensing grace. All His children are not led in one and the same way. Some must drink of the bitter waters of Marah while others may recline beneath the palm trees and regale on the streams which issue from the wells of Elim.... And has it pleased God to bring you over to Christ in a mild and easy way? Duty demands that you give Him the praise for having drawn you with the cords of love without feeling that indescribable anguish which has embittered the lives of other Christians for months, yes, for years."

This young man had not arbitrarily selected this passage, but rather, it unexpectedly confirmed the instruction the Lord Himself had just given him. This opened the way for him to the Lord's Table—and yet, on Saturday evening he stood before me. He was so afraid that he might deceive himself, so afraid that he would eat and drink judgment to himself. So much was militating against him.

After having told him that I would not dare to exclude him if the Lord had given him freedom to partake, he departed. According to his own testimony, the next morning it was as if he were brought to the Lord's Table, seeing no one but the Lord alone. It became an unforgettable day for him, myself, and others.

Never measure yourself and others by the extraordinary experiences of someone else. It will cause unnecessary anxiety. Experiences that in all simplicity align with the Holy Scriptures, not extraordinary ones, are characteristic of genuine grace.

A lady experienced something much like this young man experienced. Here is her account, taken from her letter:

> When it was hopeless from my side and I thought that I would be cast away from before the Lord's countenance, my eyes were opened for Christ, the Mighty One upon whom the Lord has laid help. This happened when a sermon was preached on the text, "How shall I put thee among the children, and give thee a pleasant land?" Then it was also possible for me. Not too long after this, the minister preached a preparatory sermon for the Lord's Supper. How my heart was stirred within me! But yet, this was not for me. That was for God's people. Furthermore, the change in me had been so gradual. The knowledge of my sins was insufficient; I had not truly mourned over my guilt, etc. I had begun with myself.
>
> It was a week full of strife and unbelief. It finally caused me to cry out, "Lord, wilt Thou Thyself declare to me whether the initiative was mine or Thine? Oh grant that I will not deceive myself." It was then that these words came to mind in such a sweet fashion: "I drew them with cords of a man, with bands of love." The most wonderful thing, however, was that I could believe that I was one of them.
>
> Immediately, I began to search in my Bible whether these words were to be found there, for otherwise it would not be true. Finally I found them in

Hosea 4:11a, and thus I had not deceived myself. I had received an answer from the Lord—on Saturday.

When, however, the minister administered the Lord's Supper that Sunday, I had such respect for that man that I did not dare to go to the first table. It was then that these words came to my mind, "Why do you fear a man who shall become as stubble?" With trembling, and being full of fear, I went to the second table. What a disappointment this was! I had expected that the Lord Jesus would reveal Himself to me and that in some measure I would experience His presence. It was darker within me than ever before. It was as if I felt Satan pounce on me, saying, "You have eaten and drunk judgment to yourself." I do not know how I got home. I could not stay inside. When, however, I stood behind our house, overcome by despair, it resounded within my heart, "Though it tarry, wait for it; because it will surely come, it will not tarry" (Hab. 2:3). I felt a sense of relief. However, I did not hear much of the sermon later that day. I was so tired and exhausted.

On Monday, the minister preached elsewhere, and mentioned in his sermon that the Lord's Supper had been administered the previous day, and that some had possibly partaken who had no right to do so. That hit home with me. Once more I was deeply discouraged. On Wednesday a seminary student was scheduled to preach, and I went to hear him. Perhaps the Lord would yet be pleased to instruct me. While driving my bike, I passed two women who were conversing together. The one, a God-fearing woman, asked me to stop and said, "You dare to take big steps. I would like you to tell me how this went." However, I was not able to do so. When I told her that I was on my way to church, she let me go with the words, "And yet, I would like to know more about it."

The seminary student preached about these words, "Him that cometh to me I will in no wise cast out" (John 6:37b). After I came home from church, I wrote a letter to the woman I previously referred to and placed it in her mailbox. It was during the sermon of this seminary student that I could believe that the Lord Jesus would also not cast me out. This was a great wonder to me, and I was able to communicate this to her. This gave me relief, but as Sunday approached, I was more despondent than before. On Sunday morning there was a voice within that said, "Don't bother going to church; for you it is hopeless anyway. You might as well end your life."

After much strife, I nevertheless dressed myself to go to church. I arrived late, and the congregation was singing already. They were singing,

> *When the needy seek Him,*
> *He will mercy show;*
> *Yea, the weak and helpless*
> *Shall His pity know;*
> *He will surely save them*
> *From oppression's might,*
> *For their lives are precious*
> *In His holy sight.*
> — Psalter 200:2
> Psalm 72:12–13

I was overwhelmed when I heard this. That morning, it was as if there was a church service for me only. The sermon fully addressed my circumstances. It was almost identical to what I had written in my letter and to what I had experienced. It became very clear to me that I had not deceived myself, but that the Lord had also invited me to His Table. I could not get over it. When afterwards I walked on a lonely road, I sang audibly, "My mouth shall sing for aye Thy tender mercies, Lord" (Psalter 422:1). Someone said subsequently that I was a bit presumptuous in singing this. However, at that moment my heart was overflowing. It was such a wonder for me that I could not do otherwise.

The Lord did, however, take this away from me, showing me more and more of myself so that again I viewed myself as an outsider, being constantly plagued with the idea that my beginning was not sound.

The young man who was privileged to experience such a blessed celebration of the Lord's Supper also encountered much strife. During the evening following this unforgettable Sunday, he had read about the wise builder who built his house upon a rock. While he was reading, the question arose whether the house of his hope was founded upon the rock—whether he was united to the Rock, that is, Christ. Could he say that Christ was his portion, and did he indeed belong to Christ? Though he could not deny that Christ had become precious to him, and that he neither could, dared to, nor wished to take refuge anywhere else except in Christ, yet neither could he say that Christ was his portion. He missed this, and to miss Christ would be to miss everything. As a result, this young man became very distressed. He prayed, but his prayer returned unto his own heart. This distress prompted him to turn to the Bible for instruction, but it was like a sealed book for him. He told me that he panicked. He was overcome by anxiety, and in a state of despair he came to me.

After listening to this young man speak haltingly, with sentences sometimes interspersed with lengthy pauses, I asked him a few questions. After inquiring how he ended up in this situation, I asked him whether on that Sunday and the day following he thought he had "arrived" in regard to his appropriation of what the Lord Jesus merited and the Lord covenantally bequeaths to His church.

For a moment, a smile came on the anxious face of this young man. He readily confessed that such had been the case. My response initially puzzled him a great deal, for I congratulated him. When he asked me why I did so, I responded by saying, "With the fact that the Lord has kept you from resting upon that which was merely meant to be an encouragement to persevere in pressing 'toward the mark for the prize of the high calling of God'" (Phil. 3:14). He had made a wrong application and a wrong use of the encouraging experiences he had during and after the administration of the Lord's Supper. And he was neither the first nor the last who had done so.

I recognized this faulty thinking from my own experience and that of others. Would there be a single child of God who would have never erred in this respect?

I cannot tell you how happy I was that the Lord immediately confronted the young man with what he was missing! The Lord can bestow a blessing on these people—not upon people who, in their own estimation, have "arrived." "He hath filled the hungry with good things" (Luke 1:53).

After I had shown this young man from God's Word that he had not deceived himself in his expectations of the Lord, but rather, had been misguided in his interpretation of his experiences, he departed. "What a great fool I am!" was the last thing he said. I also congratulated him with the fact that he arrived at that conclusion! I then availed myself of the opportunity to direct him to the One who said, "If any of you lack wisdom, let him ask of God, that giveth to all men liberally, and upbraideth not; and it shall be given him" (James 1:5). However painful it may be, it must nevertheless be viewed as a blessing when those who overextend themselves spiritually are immediately corrected. If only this would happen more frequently! When digging for the foundation of our hope (as the wise builder did), we are so inclined to rest in the act of digging. This inhibits growth in the grace and knowledge of the Lord Jesus Christ—growth whereby we acquire the subjective and conscious union with Christ as the foundation of our hope.

In His wisdom and love, the Lord commanded that

there should be six Cities of Refuge in Israel. These cities functioned as havens of refuge so that within their gates those who were fleeing from the avenger of death could be delivered from a certain death (Num. 35). These cities are rightfully viewed as exemplifying Christ who is the true City of Refuge, for "there is...no condemnation to them which are in Christ Jesus" (Rom. 8:1).

By fleeing to Christ as the City of Refuge, fearing the just wrath of God because of sin, and being deeply convinced that there is only one place of safety (that is, in the City of Refuge, Christ), we are on the right pathway. Through His Word and sacraments, the Lord confirms to those who humbly seek their purification and salvation outside of themselves in Christ Jesus that the persevering seekers of the liberty to be found in Christ shall also become finders. It is inexpressibly great when someone, by the appropriating and Spirit-wrought grace of God, experientially takes hold of God's promise that those who seek shall find (as was true for the young man referred to above). However, this does not mean that such a person is already in the City of Refuge. The Lord does not want us to view the promise of finding as one and the same as the act of finding itself. He does not want us to find rest outside of the City of Refuge. We are naturally inclined to be seekers of false rest, but God promotes His glory and our salvation by leading us to the knowledge of finding rest in the City of Refuge (1 Cor. 1:30).

Though it is true that in regard to divine election and the redemptive work of Christ, the drawing, running, seeking, and finding of the sinner are inseparably connected, it is nevertheless evident that there is a distinction between seeking and finding—both of which must be known for salvation. The Lord has given many promises to those who are running to the City of Refuge, such as, "Your heart shall live that seek God" (Ps. 69:32). The purpose of such promises is to encourage and strengthen the runners in the race, but not that they should rest in them.

We will always do well to give heed to what the apostle Paul wrote in 1 Corinthians 9:24–27: "Know ye not that they which run in a race run all, but one receiveth the prize? So run, that ye may obtain. And every man that striveth for the mastery is temperate in all things. Now they do it to obtain a corruptible crown; but we an incorruptible. I therefore so run, not as uncertainly; so fight I, not as one that beateth the air: but I keep under my body, and bring it into subjection: lest that by any means, when I have preached to others, I myself should be a castaway." Satan and our sinful hearts conspire and work together to prompt us to rest when, instead, we ought to make haste and flee for our life's sake. Regretfully, they so often succeed! However, to the glory of God's grace, He that has begun a good work in His own shall see to it that they, by His Word and providence, shall time and again be kept from a false rest so that one will instead give heed to His exhortation to make haste. In doing so, the Lord will not spare our flesh and blood! It was to the benefit of this young man that he experienced this.

Subsequently, this young man also experienced that by taking away the former, the Lord would also grant him something else in its place that would yield more steadfastness in the Lord.

When the Lord takes something away from His children, He does not do so to irritate them. In order to receive more out of the fullness of Christ and to rest solely in that in which God rests—namely, the one sacrifice of Christ—it is initially and progressively necessary for the Lord to empty us and make room for this rest. That this process neither is nor can be without strife is rooted in the fact that no one is willing to have that taken from him which he holds to be valuable. Though we may intellectually understand that this is both profitable and necessary for us, our flesh and blood will object when the Lord deems it necessary to remove it. Moreover, Satan, the world, and self—a self that cherishes a false rest—resist the Lord's ways to the uttermost.

Happily, the Lord upholds His own cause and honor, and He promotes the salvation of His own in spite of all opposition and resistance —regardless of where this originates. His Name shall eternally be magnified, regardless of all opposition from within and without!

How the Lord's ways differ in accomplishing the salvation of sinners! One person is led immediately to the edge of the abyss, whereas others will be allured and thereafter will be brought into the wilderness (Hos. 2:14). But consider this. Parents who have several children know that individual children cannot all be treated in identical fashion. Each child needs to be treated in accord with his character and unique circumstances. The fact that one child is treated and handled differently from another is often misinterpreted by the other children of the family. People outside of the family frequently misjudge parental conduct. Both love and wisdom require at times that some persons need to be subjected to "tough love." However, the same love and wisdom dictate that others who also deserve to be treated with "tough love" are nevertheless treated in a gentle and kind manner.

Now, He who is the embodiment of love and wisdom knows with infallible precision what is needed to bring sinners to the way of righteousness and to keep them on it. It even happens that the Lord at one time will deal gently with one of His children, and at other times more harshly. What man would have the audacity to prescribe to Him the manner in which He deals with us? What man is capable of judging whether either a tough or gentle approach is correct and most profitable? Is it not a manifestation of "desiring to be as God" that engenders such narrow-minded views that have wreaked so much havoc? How we ought to learn from Scripture (which knows of no such narrow-mindedness), to accept, appreciate, and admire diversity!

Narrow-mindedness is the fruit of ignorance, and ignorance is the mother of heresy. Moreover, he who seeks to impose his narrow-minded views on others is guilty of lording it over God's heritage. This is both abominable and objectionable. He who is guilty of this invokes the displeasure of God. By such grieving of God's Spirit, he will bring spiritual darkness and leanness upon himself. Such grieving of the Spirit occurs when we oppose and resist the Lord in our own life—and it also occurs when we resist and even oppose the Lord's work in others.

They who complain about spiritual darkness or leanness ought to earnestly examine themselves before the countenance of the Lord whether this could possibly be the cause of their condition. Narrow-mindedness is not a fruit of the Spirit—much less the tendency to impose one's views or experiences upon others.

In the allegorical and instructive booklet of Pleun Klein, *The Five Porches of Bethesda*, written to give guidance to the godly in the various stages of spiritual life, "harsh" Peter is not held in very high esteem. The writer was a gracious man who had received a special gift to comfort the feebleminded (1 Thess. 5:14). While still a young man, I was a frequent witness of this. His gift of spiritual discretion was universally acknowledged among the godly. His allegorical approach, evident in his books, was accepted with a charitable spirit. He abhorred narrow-mindedness in ministering to souls, which is evident in the aforementioned book—a book that has been a blessing for many.

Shortly before his death at a very ripe, old age, I visited him. He was bed-ridden. He knew that the Lord's Supper would be administered the next Lord's Day in our congregation in Rotterdam. Though he was not a member of the congregation, he confided in me that he had such a longing to show forth the death of the Lord in the midst of the congregation on the coming Lord's Day, "for," he said, "in His death alone is life."

Even though this man had learned much from the Lord, had experienced much of the Lord's salvation, and was a seasoned child of God, he was nevertheless so small in himself. His hope was not rooted in what he had experienced, for he could not face death with what had happened in his own life. He could only face death on the basis of what had happened in the life of the Lord Jesus, hoping and leaning upon His grace.

He did not underestimate what the Lord had granted him out of the fullness of Christ. On the contrary! As proof of having been adopted by God as His son—by grace and for Christ's sake—he deemed his experiences most valuable. However, they were not the foundation of his hope. The sacrifice of Christ, accomplished on the cross, was the sole foundation of his hope. He had learned experientially to lose all foundations outside of this sacrifice, and to cast the anchor of his hope in this ground. However, though his anchor was securely fastened, the ship of his life was not always in calm waters. At times, his ship was greatly buffeted by waves! Some did not understand this, thinking that a man who had received so much grace would be exempt from this.

He once said to me in a manner so characteristic of himself, "People are always thinking too highly of me. This is detrimental for me." He was also dependent on God's gracious provision, time and again. He was still in the battlefield. He still struggled with unbelief and doubts. It was his desire to encourage himself in the Lord His God by way of the Lord's Supper. It was his desire that, by way of this sacrament, his faith that salvation is the Lord's would be strengthened, that He would finish perfectly what He had undertaken for him, and that He would also grant him the victory for His covenant's sake.

No, his book confirms that Mr. Klein was neither a harsh nor a haughty man. His heart was especially drawn to the little ones in grace, and his desire was to assist them in their spiritual battle. He abhorred people who thought highly of themselves. Such people are generally also very harsh. They think so highly of themselves and their experiences that they oppress the little ones in grace, rather than encourage them. Once such a haughty person visited Pleun Klein. At a given moment, Mr. Klein said to this captain of a freighter, "Captain, what cargo do you transport?" He responded, "Hay and straw." "That is exactly what I thought," replied Klein. "Why don't you start transporting sand? There will be more depth to your work!"

When Mr. Klein and I shook hands for the last time, he held my hand tightly. He then said to me, "Will you say to all who have fought the good fight and who love the Lord's appearance, that it shall be well with them?" I wish to use this occasion to do so!

Discussion Questions

1. Can being "drawn with cords of lovingkindness" occur outside of having experiential knowledge of being lost because of sin?

2. Does the measure of my acquaintance with my misery determine how genuine it is?

3. Can it always be attributed to the preaching we hear or the spiritual counsel we are given whether, to a greater or lesser degree, we have been led gently?

4. Should people be counseled not to read conversion stories?

5. By what standard must we judge every conversion account and experience, including our own?

6. What benefit can be derived from reading the accounts of godly men and women who were led according to the Holy Scriptures?

—7—

Always Much Strife?

Being spiritually exercised by the Lord's Supper and partaking of the Lord's table are often accompanied by much strife. A young man, after hearing discussions about such strife, recently asked me, "Must there always be so much strife? Who would be jealous of this?"

I responded that it is not true that partaking of the Lord's Supper is *always* accompanied by much strife. The Lord knows precisely what someone can bear and what we each need. He will not try us above and beyond what we are able to handle. It often *appears* that our trials do exceed our strength to endure them, but He will give us a cross in proportion to our strength and strength in proportion to our cross.

Why then is there often so much strife? It is the full intent of Satan and his cohorts—the powers of the air and the carnal lusts of the flesh (even within us)—to keep those for whom the Lord instituted His Supper from partaking at His table.

The Lord is pleased at times to permit temptations and satanic influences without and within to assault His people. He will determine both the measure and the time. He may permit His people to experience such a measure of strife that, experiencing their complete helplessness and dependency, they will truly need the Lord. He does so in order that they would adore and thank Him in a more heartfelt manner for His wonderful help and assistance.

Without strife, there will be no victory *through* Him; without victory, there will be no crown *from* Him; and without that crown, there will also be no glorying *in* Him for receiving that crown.

Thus, all things are of Him, through Him, and unto Him (Rom. 11:36), and all things must "work together for good to them that love God and are the called according to his purpose" (Rom. 8:28).

Understandably, we do not relish strife. Even those who can echo the poet of Psalm 119—that "it is good for me to have been afflicted.... I know...that thou in faithfulness hast afflicted me...that I might learn thy statutes" (vv. 71–75)—will shrink from new trials. They know firsthand that, in order to experience God's grace, help, and assistance, we have to encounter circumstances in which we need such grace, help, and assistance.

Yet, was not even the Lord Jesus Himself troubled when the hour of His final and deepest suffering in soul and body came (John 12:27–29)? Was He not troubled in spirit when the moment arrived that He would be betrayed (John 13:21)? He knew that this betrayal would take place, for it had already been prophesied by David (Ps. 41). Willingly, He agreed to suffer all that was requisite to the accomplishment of God's good pleasure—He had agreed to die on the cross. And yet, when the climax of all this approached, He was greatly affected. He was troubled and filled with a sense of dread, all without sinning. He therefore turned to His heavenly Father in prayer, seeking His help and assistance, doing so in many a night, both in Jerusalem (John 12:27) and in Gethsemane (Luke 22:39–45). If even the sinless One at times dreaded His approaching suffering, how much more frequently will that be the case with us!

The wonder of God's regenerating grace is that a believer not only begins to delight in the recompense of the reward, but also in the way that leads to this reward. We read of Moses that he chose "rather to suffer affliction with the people of God, than to enjoy the pleasures of sin for a season; esteeming the reproach of Christ greater riches than the treasures in Egypt: for he had respect unto the recompence of the reward" (Heb. 11:25-26). By nature, strife is not appealing to anyone. At best, people will desire the crown but not the cross. Yet, no one will wear a crown of glory who has not been a bearer of the cross of Christ in some measure. Did not all those who are before the throne come out of great tribulation, having washed their robes and made them white in the blood of the Lamb (Rev. 7:14)? Is it not written that God's children must enter into the kingdom of God through much tribulation (Acts 14:22)? None of us would be inclined to choose the way of tribulation and strife. However, what is impossible for our corrupt nature is possible by God's grace and power. He makes salvation (the recompense of the reward) so desirable that our wills are inclined toward whatever God calls us to do in order to become a partaker of His salvation, no matter what this may entail. We read therefore that "godly sorrow worketh repentance to salvation not to be repented of" (2 Cor. 7:10). It is understandable that no one will be jealous of the strife of God's people. However, without such strife, there would be no experiences of God's salvation of which someone can be jealous indeed. The one is inseparably connected to the other.

Granted, not all of God's children experience strife in an equal measure. There are those who enter into the kingdom of heaven without having known much strife. God alone can determine in what measure one must strive to enter into the narrow gate. No one should question his spiritual state due to having experienced either much or little strife. Instead, everyone should examine himself whether he knows something of fighting the good fight fought by all who are saved.

In this context, I wish to repeat what I have stated earlier: Never measure yourself and others by the extraordinary circumstances of someone else's life. Such comparisons bring about unnecessary anxiety. The extraordinary is not the mark of genuine experience, but rather, that which is according to Holy Scripture in all its simplicity. No one ought to wish for the same measure of strife as another believer may have experienced. Rather, everyone should long for the ministry of God's Spirit in order that he might be, and continue to be, desirous to fear the Lord.

> *Who is he that fears Jehovah,*
> *Walking with Him day by day?*
> *God will lead him safely onward,*
> *Guide him in the chosen way.*
> —Psalter 415:6

Therefore, desire neither misery nor despondency, but rather, clarity and integrity.[1]

They who fear the Lord must see to it that they do not speak only about their strife, but also about the experience of God's mercy, particularly in the presence of small children, young people, and beginners in grace. Be on guard against fostering the notion that the service of the Lord only consists of misery and strife. An experienced child of God, long since deceased, once said to her friend, "My misery I tell to the Lord, but to people I speak about how good the Lord is for sinful people."

When someone experiences much strife, it can be very good and beneficial to point out to them from Scripture, and possibly from one's own experience, that this is not a strange matter; but we must learn when and to whom to

---

1. This is the translation of the Dutch adage: "Sta niet naar naarheid of zwaarheid, maar naar klaarheid en waarheid."

say it. What is good for one person may be detrimental to another.

To address those problems that occur prior to, during, and after partaking of the Lord's Supper, let me detail another incident from one of my former congregations.

After having partaken of the Lord's Supper for the first time in her life, a member was overjoyed. She experienced much strife, but the Scripture that had been expounded and applied prior to the administration of the Lord's Supper so affected her that she came to the table with Esther's disposition: "If I perish, I perish" (Esther 4:16). Upon coming, she took refuge in the King of kings to "obtain mercy, and find grace to help in time of need" (Heb. 4:16). Just as the king extended the golden scepter of peace to Esther, this woman experienced likewise that grace is poured into the lips of Zion's king. She was privileged to experience the rest that remains for the people of God in this life—a foretaste of the eternal Sabbath rest. Her partaking of the table of the covenant turned out well for her. She was amazed that the Lord was so good for sinful people.

At the next administration of the Lord's Supper, she again took a seat at the table. As she sat, however, she became very unsettled. She experienced nothing of what she experienced the first time. This made her fearful that she had eaten and drunk judgment to herself; she questioned herself, whether she had merely imagined the previous experience and whether all she thought she had received from the Lord had in fact been self-deception.

She returned home that day in a state of great confusion and anxiety. Due to her spiritual distress, she did not know how she would get supper prepared. She tried to hide her state of mind. While sighing and crying out to the Lord for mercy, she did manage to put the meal on the table, but she, herself, could hardly eat, due to her inner distress. At the conclusion of the meal, the Bible was brought to the table. She feared the worst, namely, that the reading of the scheduled portion of Scripture would yield her death sentence. She could not deny that this would be just. The portion read was Revelation 3. Upon hearing the words, "Thou hast a little strength, and hast kept my word, and hast not denied my name" (Rev. 3:8), she was suddenly delivered from her bondage. How wholeheartedly she concurred that she had but little strength!

She told me later that it was also greatly comforting to her that she perceived that the Lord knew everything about her circumstances. Though she was ashamed that she had been so "void of strength and prone to stumble" (Psalter 444:5), yet it encouraged her to know that the Lord knew her frame. It was a great wonder to her that the Lord in His mercy did not reject her because of her frailty.

By way of the words, "Thou...hast kept my word, and hast not denied my name," it also dawned on her that by her eating of the bread and drinking of the wine at the Lord's Table in remembrance of Him, she kept His Word and had not denied His Name. Whatever she did not receive at the table, she received at home: the Lord's approbation on her partaking of the Lord's Supper. Unspeakable joy and wonder filled her heart after enduring hours of distress.

However, the instruction she received regarding the causes of the great confusion she had experienced was the more enduring blessing.

The first matter she was led to understand had to do with the purpose of the Lord's Supper. She realized that we do not attend the Lord's table primarily to receive something, but rather, to confess something: that we have found death in all that is not Christ, and seek life outside of ourselves in Christ. How worthy the Lord is of being obeyed and honored, even though there would be no gracious reward associated with it! "Who is there even among you that would shut the doors for nought? neither do ye kindle fire on mine altar for nought" (Mal. 1:10). Is the focus on us or on Him when showing forth the death of the Lord? Is *our* interest or *His* interest of central importance? Does love for the Lord, His institution, and His honor motivate us in our partaking of the Lord's Supper, or is it selfish love?

These are questions that we must diligently consider as we prepare ourselves for the Lord's Supper. Partaking of the Lord's Supper is about showing forth His death rather than the seeking of His reward (be it a gracious reward). It is the confession of His Name, as well as the public acknowledgement that our hope is in His Name alone, which must be our objective in attending. We must be motivated by our desire to keep His Word, by reverential obedience of His command of love ("This do in remembrance of me"), and by taking refuge in faith to the Mediator between God and man. When other impure, unholy motives dominate over holy motives, we will dwell in a dry land. How much we must unlearn things in the Kingdom of God in order to learn the holy art of living a life that is pleasing to the Lord!

Were it not so that the heavenly Prophet Christ would accomplish this by His Spirit, there would be no one who would pursue this. Without realizing it, this woman had been more concerned about herself and her advantage than the Lord and His honor.

The focal point of our partaking of the Lord's Supper should be what the German poet, Gerhard Tersteegen, expressed in his beautiful hymn "Ich bete an die Macht der Liebe" ("I worship the power of love"). In one of the stanzas of this hymn we read, "Ich will, anstatt an mich zu denken, ins Meer der Liebe mich versenken" ("Rather than thinking of myself, I wish to sink away in the sea of love").

However, there were additional difficulties that contributed to the unsettled state of mind in this woman I referenced. From the moment she arose to take her place at the Lord's Table, her attention was focused entirely upon that which was transpiring *within* her. I believe that this was the root cause of all that would follow. Rather than lifting her heart "on high in heaven where Christ Jesus is our Advocate at the right hand of His heavenly Father" (Lord's Supper Form), she was turning within and focused on what was transpiring there. Rather than casting the anchor of her hope outside herself into the unchangeable anchor ground of Jesus Christ and Him crucified, she cast the anchor of her hope into the changing ground of the internal dispositions of her life of faith. All God's children experience that this leads to misery rather than stability. She was not aware of the fact that she lived by what she *felt* rather than by what she *believed*.

The desire for the sensible, tangible experience of the Lord's salvation is inseparably connected to the life of faith. Those who do not desire the tender manifestation of the Lord's favor nor have any experiential knowledge of the Lord's salvation do not know the true life of faith. Living faith and true love desire genuine, experiential interaction with the object of their love. That is a mark of healthy spiritual life—of fainting for the courts of the Lord (Ps. 84:2). "Let him kiss me with the kisses of his mouth" and "his right hand doth embrace me" (Songs 1:2, 2:6, 8:3) are expressions in which the bride of Christ (His church in general and each child of God in particular) strikingly articulates this desire for emotional contact.

However, if the love and faithfulness of the Lord are measured and evaluated by what we feel, we are on the wrong track. The godly Andrew Gray calls this the doctrine of unbelief. How erroneous it is to determine what lives in the Lord's heart by what we see and feel of Him in the realm of His providence! That spawns unbelief and renders God suspect in His love, faithfulness, and power.

We will only trust Him insofar as we see Him and insofar as He manifests Himself to us. Is this how the Lord should be treated?

Has He ever dealt with us in a way that would justify such a suspicious evaluation of His actions? Would not every faithful husband have just cause to be angry if he were to detect such suspicion in his wife? Would not every wife be deeply offended and grieved if she were to detect such suspicion in her husband without ever having given him just cause? Should we then be surprised if the Lord hides His face when we are guilty of "trusting" Him in such a fashion? We do Him great injustice and grieve Him.

The Lord knows that faith, hope, and love are still imperfect in His children. He knows our frame and remembers that we are dust. And yet, it is His will that we trust Him and His Word. That is why He gave us His Word and instituted the sacraments. What a difficult lesson it is to learn to live by faith and not by sense!

We will no doubt stumble often as we learn to believe in hope against all hope (as Abraham and Sarah did for many years)—to believe that God is gracious and faithful, even though I neither see nor feel anything of the fulfillment of God's promises. How ashamed the disciples must have been when the Lord Jesus asked them, "Why are ye fearful, O ye of little faith?" (Matt. 8:26)! They had no answer to this, for He had never given them any reason or occasion to be fearful.

Though some children of God are more exercised in this holy art and skill, yet none of God's children on earth have ever achieved perfection in their walk of faith. Someone once stated it this way: "Here upon earth God's children will not receive a diploma for any aspect of the life of faith."

This does not mean, however, that we must not do battle against unbelief, in dependence on the Lord. This is evident from the words the Lord spoke to Thomas after His resurrection: "Be not faithless, but believing...because thou hast seen me, thou hast believed: blessed are they that have not seen, and yet have believed" (John 20:27–29).

Finally, we can identify a third cause for the confusion and distress this woman experienced at her second attendance of the Lord's table. Justus Vermeer pointed out in his exposition of the Heidelberg Catechism that the focus of the celebration of the Lord's Supper is not upon receiving the *sensible* assurance of the Lord's favor, but rather, upon the *sacramental* assurance of this. The receipt of the sensible assurance of God's favor is an added gift—a foretaste of eternal bliss. However, the Lord never promised His people that they would receive the assurance of sense with every celebration of the Lord's Supper. To love and trust a God whose love and faithfulness I feel is one thing, but to love, trust, and worship a God who hides Himself and takes away what we thought we could not live without—that is a different matter. But God uses both experiences to strengthen His people in the exercise of their most holy faith in His grace, love, and faithfulness.

What characterizes little ones in grace is that the measure in which they are assured of being the recipients of the Lord's grace and of being loved by Him fluctuates in proportion with their sensible experience of the Lord's salvation. This is different with those who are more exercised in grace. Being taught by the Spirit of the Lord out of His Word, and having experienced the application of what Christ merited for them to their soul, they have learned to deem Him faithful who has promised (Heb. 10:23), even though they cannot sense anything of His presence (Job 19:25).

The Lord instituted the sacraments to foster growth in assurance, so that His people would learn to exercise the "yet" of faith in the battle arena of life. When this woman wanted to enjoy the assurance of sense rather than sacramental assurance at the Lord's Supper, she became confused and even panicked when she did not experience the assurance of sense. She was neither the first nor the last to experience this.

Discussion Questions

1. Why do some of the godly frequently struggle spiritually just prior to the celebration of the Lord's Supper?

2. Why doesn't the Lord prevent them from having such strife?

3. Why do you think some of the godly experience more internal strife than others?

4. May the measure of strife (or the lack thereof) be a determining factor for one's partaking of the Lord's Supper?

5. Is having an emotional experience, or not having it, when partaking of the Lord's Supper a touchstone for judging whether someone's partaking of the Lord's Supper was in the Lord's favor?

6. Why is it wrong to measure the Lord's love and faithfulness by what we *feel* of these blessings?

8

He Hath Filled the Hungry
with Good Things

In one of my congregations, something remarkable happened on a Saturday morning, the day before the administration of the Lord's Supper. The previous Sunday, I had preached a preparatory sermon about these words: "Come, see a man, which told me all things that ever I did: is not this the Christ?" (John 4:29).

Let me provide the context by summarizing my sermon. I had pointed the congregation to the gracious wonder that Jesus needed to go through Samaria. There were lost sheep there who had to be brought to salvation. Utterly lost men and women in Samaria were chosen, out of sovereign and free grace, before the foundation of the world to be blessed for Christ's sake. Through Christ's Word and Spirit, they had to be regenerated. They had to be turned from darkness to light and from the power of Satan unto God that they might receive forgiveness of sins and an inheritance among those sanctified by faith in Christ (Acts 26:18).

One of those who believed, by the grace of God and through the instrumentality of His Word, was a woman with a very sinful past—a woman who testified, "We have heard him ourselves, and know that this is indeed the Christ, the Saviour of the world" (John 4:41–42). Seated at Jacob's well, the Lord Jesus had said to this woman, "Give me to drink." He initiated a conversation with her—a woman with whom many refused to have any form of fellowship due to her ungodly and offensive life-style. In His seeking love He reached out to this woman who was dead in trespasses and sins, and who being without God, Christ, and hope, lived according to the lusts of her sinful heart.

How righteously God's Son and Servant could have left her in that lost state, as He could righteously do with all of us! Though it is true that the one will indulge more in sin than the other, we are all gone out of the way, we are together become unprofitable; "there is none that doeth good, no, not one" (Rom. 3:12). It is very well possible that the people in Samaria shunned this woman because of her shameful life. People probably do not treat us as such. Would that also be the case if the sins we have committed either secretly or publicly would be known to the community? Let him who is without sin cast the first stone upon this Samaritan woman! How thankful we must be to God that His Son did not come to call the "righteous" to repentance, for then not a single human being could be saved! He came to call and save sinners. Proceeding from the eternal love of a triune God, the Lord also drew this woman out of darkness to His wonderful light. "For whatsoever doth make manifest is light" (Eph. 5:13).

The Lord confronted also this woman with her sins —as He did, does, and will do with all whom He purchased with His precious blood to be redeemed from the vain conversation which characterizes all men by nature (1 Pet. 18–19). This woman did not contradict His searching words. Later on she said, "He told me all that ever I did (John 4:39). She made no effort at all to minimize or justify her sin. All who have been made a sinner before God for the first time or by renewal experience something of what the poet of Psalm 32:5 confesses, "I acknowledged my sin unto thee, and mine iniquity have I not hid. I said, I will confess my transgressions unto the LORD." I believe that she did likewise, though we do not find these exact words in her confession.

However, the Lord Jesus did not only speak with this woman about her sins. He also spoke to her about Himself. Connecting with what the woman herself had said—"I know that Messias cometh, which is called Christ: when he is come, he will tell us all things"—He said to the woman, "I that speak unto thee am he" (John 4:25-26). From what is written in verse 28, we can learn what effect these words had upon her. The woman left her waterpot, went into the city, and said to the people, "Come, see a man, which told me all things that ever I did: is not this the Christ?" In saying, "is this not the Christ?" she did not mean to say that she still doubted this. This becomes evident from the testimony of those who said later, "Now we believe, not because of thy saying: for we have heard him ourselves, and know that this is indeed the Christ, the Saviour of the world" (v. 42). This had been her testimony indeed, for Christ Himself had said this—and thus it became the testimony of others as well. In order to accomplish this, Christ *had* to go through Samaria, so that it would be fulfilled,

> *In gladsome strains we'll hear her sons relate:*
> *These all were born within the walls of Zion.*
> — Psalter 442:3

Since Christ instituted the Lord's Table for His people and for them alone, I invited in the Lord's name all whose experience, confession, and actions were like the Samaritan woman's to partake of the meal Christ had instituted in order that the spiritually needy who believe in His name would be filled with good things.

On the Saturday morning following this sermon, something unique happened. I finished the necessary preparations for the ministry of the Word and the administration of the Lord's Supper very quickly, and I could not decide what to do with the rest of my day. This prompted me to pray, "Lord, what wilt thou have me to do?" Shortly thereafter, it came to my mind that there were some elderly members of the congregation whom I had not yet visited. I was relatively new to this congregation and had almost finished making the rounds among the seniors. I could not shake the thought that I should visit these people, and I quickly made my way to their home.

I was taken off guard when, instead of an elderly person opening the door, a young woman stood before me. With astonishment, and yet in a friendly manner, she said, "Hello, Pastor," and invited me in. I thought to myself, "This woman obviously knows me, so I had better step in." Her happy surprise in seeing me was so obviously written on her face that I dared not say that I could not come in because my intention was to visit the elderly.

After some initial dialogue, the woman suddenly said to me, "Pastor, if I have ever been compelled to believe that there is a God in heaven who hears and answers prayers, then I must believe it at this moment." She told me that the preparatory sermon of the previous Sunday had touched her deeply. What she had heard during that sermon remained with her day and night. In the history of the Samaritan woman, there were several things that resembled her own life story.

She did not have five husbands, but rather, only one, and by Christian standards she and her husband had a good marriage. However, the circumstances that culminated in their marriage were not as they ought to be. Even though she had made public confession of guilt, she continued to be plagued by guilt. Gradually, she began to feel guilty about other sins as well. She said to me, "Pastor, I became aware of all that I had ever done, and I did not know where to turn. I prayed, read, attended church as frequently as I could, and did many other things. However, my feelings of guilt increased instead of decreasing. I tried to live as holy a life as I could, but it turned out to be a dismal failure."

About the same time, a second child was born. When she was under the preaching of God's Word, it was as if light arose in her troubled soul. She was overwhelmed by the perception of Jesus' suitability and willingness to save sinners. Her heart was drawn to Him who said, "Come unto me, all ye that labour and are heavy laden, and I will give you rest" (Matt. 11:28). There was a ray of hope in her heart; perhaps it was possible for her to be saved. However, her hope did not last long. She could not believe that the holy Son of God would welcome someone with such a history as hers, with so much sin and with such a sinful heart. Nevertheless, such moments as I have just described returned from time to time.

Not long after the birth of her second child, a third child was on the way. This woman panicked. "Pastor," she said, "it was not that I did not want more children, but I didn't know how I could keep a handle on everything. I still felt so weak and tired, and I often felt so miserable." In spite of her diligent efforts to suppress them, tears ran down the face of this young mother; her oldest child could not understand why Mommy was crying. She told me that she began to think seriously about suicide. This generated new and oppressive feelings of guilt. All hope of salvation was gone. She was such a sinful woman and such a poor mother; there could be no hope for her at all. Such rebellious and sinful creatures are only worthy of hell, and it would make little difference whether she would arrive there earlier rather than later.

After some time, this rebellious frame subsided, but her feelings of guilt remained. Even though her attendance in God's house often yielded more condemnation than refreshment, she persevered in attending, and occasionally there would be a spark of hope in her heart that He who said, "He that cometh unto me I will in no wise cast out," would also be willing to receive her. She then said, "There were moments (sometimes during a sermon, and other times at home) that I would say, 'Lord, to whom shall I go? Thou hast the words of eternal life. Son of David, have mercy upon me.'"

Then the Sunday morning arrived when I preached on John 4. To partake of the Lord's Supper was such a remote possibility for her that she pushed away even the thought of attending. However, upon hearing the exposition and application of the history of the Samaritan woman, there was such power in the invitation to the Lord's Table addressed to all who turn to Him in their sins and misery that she did not know what was happening to her. There was much that drew her, and there was much that held her back. When considering her history, she could only conclude that she did not belong at the Lord's Table. Furthermore, what would the people think and say? She returned to her home in great confusion. During the week of preparation, she used the few spare moments she had to read something to examine herself. By making use of God's Word, as well as books specifically written for this purpose, she examined herself—however, to no avail. And then this Saturday morning arrived.

She had a fervent desire to speak to me, but she did not know how she could. Her husband had to work and she had to care for three little children. They did not have a telephone. She then cried out, "Lord, couldst Thou not send the pastor to me? Dost Thou not have his heart in Thy hand?" And shortly thereafter, I stood before her! You will understand that I was as amazed as she was. There was a song in my heart:

On whom but God can we rely,
The Lord our God who reigns on high,

Who condescends to see and know
The things of heav'n and earth below?
— Psalter 306:3

After speaking to her in more detail about the wondrous fact that God sent His Son into the world to save sinners, that this living Savior still delights to eat and drink with publicans and sinners, and that it is "a faithful saying, worthy of all acceptation, that Christ Jesus came into the world to save sinners" (1 Tim. 1:15), I departed. Prior to my departure, I commended her to Him whose tender mercies are manifold, and whose "lovingkindness...has ever been of old." For indeed, the Lord is ready to receive in love all who cry out, "Sins of youth remember not, nor recall my hid transgression; for Thy goodness' sake, O God, think of me in Thy compassion" (Psalter 415:3)—something so clearly taught in the parable of the prodigal son.

When I left, I asked this woman where the elderly people lived whom I intended to visit. "Oh pastor," she replied, "they live on the next level." The house's door had two doorbells—one for the lower apartment and one for the upper apartment. I had simply pushed the wrong bell! The Lord had so directed my finger that I pushed the doorbell of the apartment in which this woman lived! Truly, He will hear the needy when they cry. Nothing is too hard for Him!

The next day, this troubled woman sat at the Lord's table for the first time in her life, seeing no one but Jesus alone. Truly, He did not despise nor abhor the affliction of the afflicted (Ps. 22:24). The Lord granted her a few moments of rest for her soul, and she felt great joy in the Lord. Indeed, "He hath filled the hungry with good things; and the rich he hath sent empty away" (Luke 1:53).

Discussion Questions

1. What was the "living water" that the Lord Jesus gave to the Samaritan woman when she had asked for it?

2. How did the effect of this living water manifest itself in the Samaritan woman?

3. What is it in both the confession and the actions of the Samaritan woman that reminds us of the touchstone for self-examination in the Form for the Lord's Supper, whereby we can determine whether we belong to those for whom the Lord instituted His Supper?

4. What constitutes the Lord's "filling of the hungry with good things," particularly in relation to the blessing He bestows on them who obey His loving injunction: "This do in remembrance of me"?

9

The Rich He Hath Sent
Empty Away

On the evening of that noteworthy Saturday (referred to in
the previous chapter), I had another encounter in connection with the impending Lord's Supper. Sharing some of
the details of this meeting with you, with the Lord's blessing, could possibly be to your edification as well.

A young man, approximately twenty, came to visit me
at the parsonage. He was a professing member of a sister
congregation and had been asked to pay me a visit. His
circumstances were such that he often worshipped with
our congregation on Sunday and he frequently visited the
Lord's people. He would freely converse with them and,
consequently, some of God's people had good expectations
concerning him. The consistory had given him permission
to partake of the Lord's Supper with us several times.

During the consistory meeting preceding the administration of the Lord's Supper (the first time in my new
congregation), a consistory member raised the question
whether this young man should be given permission again
to partake of the Lord's Supper. He had his doubts about
this; he heard that this young man was greatly offended by
the preparatory message. During the preparatory sermon,
I said that the table of the Lord would be open to those
who were not strangers of what the Samaritan woman had

experienced, confessed, and done—all as a result of her encounter with the Lord Jesus.

The young man disagreed with this. He was of the opinion that what this Samaritan experienced concerning misery, deliverance, and gratitude came short of the minimum requirements for partaking of the Lord's Supper.

Since this young man had expressed his displeasure in a manner that caused great offense in the congregation, the consistory deemed it necessary to have a meeting with him prior to Sunday. He arrived that Saturday evening at the parsonage. An elder had been appointed to be present at the meeting.

I first asked this young man if it would not have been better if he, before venting his displeasure in such a public fashion, had first come to speak with me to determine if there was possibly a misunderstanding. I then asked him his own view regarding regeneration, and whom he considered to be regenerate. In order to clarify his viewpoint, he made an analogy with what transpires in the natural realm. With growing amazement, I listened to what, in his opinion, took place prior to, during, and after the birth of a child. I am the father of eight children, but much of what I heard was new to me! I concluded that what this unmarried young man considered marks of a newborn actually manifested themselves much later with our children. Some of these marks did not manifest themselves until they were toddlers, and others not until they reached teenage years!

This young man was of the opinion that the Lord desires to have fellowship at His table only with those who, with an assured confidence, have embraced Him as their Surety and Savior. He refused to make a distinction between receiving the Savior with a trembling hand and receiving Him with a steady, sure hand. He also refused to make a distinction between embracing the Lord Jesus as Prophet, as the Samaritan woman had done by grace, and the saving embrace of Him as Priest and King—something that often occurs later. He believed that such embracing of the Lord Jesus as Prophet as manifested in the Samaritan woman was not sufficient for partaking of the Lord's Supper.

I pointed out that the disciples with whom the Lord Jesus celebrated the first Lord's Supper had also not yet embraced Him as Priest. They were entirely blind to His Priesthood and had no knowledge of taking refuge and trusting in Him as Priest for their justification. They completely misunderstood His Kingship as it relates to sanctification. And yet, the Lord Jesus gave them the signs and seals of their justification through His blood, their sanctification by His righteousness and power, and their glorification by His faithfulness. Are we permitted to establish different benchmarks?

Whatever arguments I used from the Holy Scriptures to persuade this young man of his error were to no avail. He insisted that only knowing, receiving, and trusting in the Lord Jesus is saving and manifests itself in trusting in Him as Surety and Mediator—and thus as Priest.

When he refused to listen to either my or the elder's arguments, I took refuge to an old writer for whom the young man claimed to have great respect. Since my acquaintance with Alexander Comrie, as well as my own experience, taught me that this young man was neither the first nor the last who was of such an opinion, I wish to share with you what I quoted from Comrie.

Many writings of this deceased servant of God (d. 1774), to whom the Lord had given more than ordinary gifts to serve and edify His church, have been published. One of these writings is his exposition of Lord's Days 1–7 of the Heidelberg Catechism, of which Rev. G. H. Kersten stated that it was much loved by God's people and provided an ongoing source of instruction and comfort. Concerning this exposition, Rev. Kersten wrote in September 1938:

"With great liberty I recommend this precious work to the reader. I especially wish to urge our young people to make a serious study of this exposition of the Catechism, so that their footsteps may be established in the Word of God, and they may recognize and wholeheartedly reject the many errors of our day."

I read something to this young man from Comrie's exposition of the seventh Lord's Day, which has had a great impact on both my personal life and my official ministry. I was hopeful that this would persuade him to change his mind.

The question is asked what true, saving faith is. Since the Lord's Supper has been instituted for true believers only, the answer is of great significance.

In explaining what the essence of saving faith is, Comrie endeavored to make it clear that saving faith does not begin when one consciously embraces Christ.

In his exposition of the Heidelberg Catechism (Utrecht: De Banier, 1941) he writes:

> Faith, as the primary and most essential means whereby we are regenerated, is granted at that specific moment when one becomes a partaker of the new nature. However, the act of faith reaches its perfection only gradually—from less to more, and from weaker to stronger. All the means of grace, such as the Word, prayer, the preaching of the Word, the sacraments, and the gathering of the saints, are used by the Holy Spirit to establish us in our faith. If this were to be understood correctly, the entire conduct of those who examine someone's conversion account to determine whether their motives truly proceed from faith, and then to either approve or disapprove of such an account, would cease. Oh, why do we quench the Spirit in ourselves and others? An important reason for this is that we are not exercised in the word of

righteousness, and consequently we do not discern matters as we ought to.

Instead, everyone would receive his appropriate portion and would be encouraged to persevere, and his deficiency would not lead him to become discouraged and passive. Rather, there would be a striving to obtain that which is needed to fulfill his need.

Subsequent to this quote, we read:

It is therefore evident that we are justified upon being grafted into Christ (which occurs at the moment of regeneration). Consequently, faith, whereby one is grafted in and justified, must be viewed in like manner—that is, not as a deed that yields the one and a passive acquiescence of the other, but rather, as an inwrought propensity toward both. This enables us to receive the grace of God in Christ Jesus, and upon such a reception, this becomes a reality. However, I need to state first of all that one's objective justification by faith (faith being the instrumental cause), is so perfect in God's tribunal that this occurs once and for all and without repetition.

According to Comrie and Colossians 2:13, this occurs at regeneration: "And you, being dead in your sins and the uncircumcision of your flesh, hath he quickened together with him, having forgiven you all trespasses." However, this union with Christ, as a consequence of such inwrought faith, will become increasingly secure and intimate due to the spiritual exercises proceeding from this inwrought faith. Such believers, who are grafted into Christ, will, so to speak, daily and increasingly be united in and to Him. We observe this in a branch that has been grafted into the stem. The attachment becomes stronger and stronger, and the branch, as it were, becomes one with it. This will lead us to understand what it is that distinguishes the prayer of believers. They do not pray that they might increasingly be justified in God's tribunal, but rather, they pray daily that they may increasingly and more intimately be united with Christ. And thus Paul sought to increasingly apprehend that for which he was apprehended (Phil. 3:13).

To clarify what has just been stated, and to prevent misunderstanding, remember that, when Comrie speaks of objective or *actual* justification, he does not mean to say that justification comes about by way of *our* actions or deeds. Rather, he understands this to mean that God actively imputes Christ's work, whereby the unrighteous, unrepentant, unbelieving sinner is declared righteous in God's sight. On the basis of this and as a fruit thereof, the sinner is quickened, renewed, and rendered capable of believing by the Holy Spirit, and will begin to repent. In harmony with the Lord's testimony in His Word, Comrie declares correctly that everything depends on this objective justification. This determines my state both now and eternally.

Rev. G. H. Kersten has also strongly emphasized this in his exposition of Lord's Day 17 of the Heidelberg Catechism. You should read and re-read this to understand its truth and meaning.

Comrie rightly states that all the ministrations of the Holy Spirit whereby we become poor in spirit, mournful, etc. (Matt. 5:1–11) are both the proof and fruit of this objective justification. When the Lord addresses the righteous in His Word, encouraging and comforting them, He is not speaking only to those who, by God's gracious revelation to them, are conscious of their being just before God. In the Beatitudes, did Jesus only pronounce those blessed who are assured within their hearts that they are righteous before God? Are not those who, to their grief and sorrow, still lack this assurance, also comforted by being assured that they are blessed and that they will be comforted at God's appointed time?

The Holy Spirit's work in assuring of real and personal justification is founded entirely upon this objective justification (as it occurred at regeneration)—a work that He accomplishes by means of His witness in the Word, in the sacraments, and in the heart. Comrie, as do many others, calls the receipt of this assurance in one's conscience subjective or *passive* justification; it has also been called "justification in the court of one's conscience."

God's Word tells us that we will not attain such assurance except upon, and following, a believing reception of Christ. In proportion to being exercised in the knowledge of misery, deliverance, and gratitude (by the operations of the Holy Spirit), believers will acquire knowledge of how God sees them in Christ Jesus.

Entering into that rest by faith is not the *essence* of faith, but the *benefit* or profit of faith. It is the *fulfillment* of God's promises, which are sacramentally signified and sealed in the sacraments to all true believers who are righteous before God in Christ. This is true for the "little ones" in grace, as well as those who are more exercised—thus regardless of the measure in which they have been exercised in the act of believing and receiving. From God's perspective, no one is more justified or less than another. It is not one's passive or subjective justification, but rather, objective justification that is the basis on which God deals with regenerated sinners. Comrie emphasized this strongly in the section I read to this young man on this given Saturday evening. All that I have written thus far has been to avoid misunderstanding regarding this quote.

Comrie writes as follows:

> This is meant as an antidote against those notions whereby the doctrine of justification is seriously undermined. This particularly relates to the manner in which so many poor souls are treated. As a result,

the Spirit is quenched, and the smoking flaxes and bruised reeds are trampled upon and squelched.

Such souls are told that all that precedes the conscious reception of faith is at best a common work with which they will perish. Such contrite souls are taught that before they receive life out of Christ they must first go to Christ and receive Him, and that thereby they receive life and a new nature. They will be told whereof such believing reception consists, and what flows out of it. Such matters make a great impression upon tender and concerned beginners in grace, since they have some knowledge of the deceitfulness of their hearts, and how grievous it would be indeed if they were to deceive themselves. Thus they reject all that they have experienced, considering it their own work. They become fixated with the act of believing itself, and have developed such notions concerning this that they are wise enough to know what it is without ever having exercised it.

We will neither investigate where nor ask from whom this manner of dealing with souls originates, which is done under the pretext of great tenderness and carefulness. I am certain that when we compare Scripture with Scripture, this is neither rooted in the Word of God, nor was it taught in former times by faithful ministers and the godly. Rather, it is a new invention. Wherever this surfaces, experience has taught me to observe two things—both here and elsewhere. On the one hand, the exercises and seriousness of some are utterly extinguished, proving by hindsight that they never possessed this inwrought propensity of faith. In others I have observed that they live with such wretchedness and strife, that they never give God the honor for what He has done in them, nor do they endeavor to gradually come to a higher level of maturity, but insist on immediately attaining to the highest level of maturity. When they do not attain this, they become, with God's permission and due to wrong teaching, tormentors of their own souls. Thereby they render the sweet first principles of the Spirit in themselves suspect, and as co-laborers of Satan ensnare their souls in the bondage of unbelief, so that no one can persuade them otherwise. It is even so that they who, according to the prudence of the saints, wish to treat them with discretion, are suspected of being too blind, unfaithful, and loveless; that is, as if they were daubing with untempered mortar and healing the wound lightly.

My soul does not wish to identify with those who suppress the first stirrings of God's work by saying to such poor worms, "Thus and thus it must be, or else it is suspect...."

On the other hand, experience has taught me that the notion I am here confronting has spawned the emergence of a group of pedantic individuals who are void of the genuine experience of the depths into which poor and needy souls can come (for God's seed must often suffer as winter wheat). Year in and year out they haughtily speak of nothing else but the guilt they have contracted, and with which they come to Christ and receive Him—and nothing more. This is their circular argument, and if one can speak of this, and one can demonstrate that he has had some spiritual stirrings, then such are the people who truly understand the way. They act as if the way to heaven only consists of a making use of Christ for the removal of the guilt of sin, and nothing else. Humble, small, and smoking flaxes hear this, and end up in the depths, not knowing what to think of this.

My beloved, if we but understood the Word of God and also our doctrine, we would be fully convinced that there can be no initiative to turn to God and Christ from the sinner who is dead in trespasses and sins. As there can be no spiritual activity prior to being grafted into Christ, also the extrinsic acts of the soul toward God and Christ issue forth from being grafted into Him, and will furnish infallible proofs of the truth and genuineness of the faith whereby one is grafted into Christ. If one were thus to give God the honor for the grace received, and would pursue both increase and growth in grace—and thus from being a child seek to become a young man, and from a young man a grown man, and from a grown man a father—one would not doubt the genuineness of his spiritual state, for one does not achieve the highest level in but a wink. Would it not be utter foolishness that one would doubt the humanity of a natural child simply because it is not yet a grown man or a father? Such is also the case here.

Though I thus tried to prove to this young man where he disagreed with Comrie, he clung to his initial view. No matter how the elder and I sought to persuade him of his error, it was to no avail.

The arguments this young man advanced gave me an opportunity to ask him a few questions about how he arrived at his opinion. This examination was obviously not restricted to merely inquiring about his intellectual knowledge. Since this young man presented himself as someone possessing spiritual life, and was received as such, I deemed it my duty to inquire about his personal spiritual life.

Upon answering my questions as to how he had acquired his knowledge experientially (and thus by the Holy Spirit having applied God's Word to him), we soon concluded that this intelligent and eloquent young man did not have a leg to stand on. He had some knowledge from reading and conversations, some impressions under the ministry of the Word, some changes in his lifestyle, and that was all. His application of Christ and His work to himself, his appropriation of this, and what he told us concerning how he acquired this knowledge gave us reason to warn him seriously. Even that he did not accept from us.

The next morning, he sat like a stone in church during the administration of the Lord's Supper, whereas the woman I wrote about in the previous chapter showed much tenderness of heart.

Shortly thereafter, circumstances in the private life of this young man resulted in him no longer frequenting our congregation. Some time later, I was told that he had abandoned all religion.

May the cases of this woman and this young man be to our learning. "Jehovah looketh from on high with kindly eye upon the lowly, but knoweth those from far who hide, in sinful pride, their ways unholy" (Psalter 429:3). "He hath filled the hungry with good things; and the rich he hath sent empty away" (Luke 1:53).

Discussion Questions

1. What are the biblical marks of regeneration?

2. What constitutes faith in the Lord Jesus Christ as Prophet, Priest, and King? By which fruits does this faith manifest itself?

3. Knowing the Lord Jesus as Prophet, and believing in Him as such, preceded the disciples' believing in Him as Priest and King. Is that still the case when the Lord leads His people to the knowledge of salvation?

4. Is it true that, when we speak of progressive growth in spiritual life, we are guilty of dissecting spiritual life in a scholastic and mystical fashion?

5. When is a sinner justified in an objective sense?

6. What does the term "passive or subjective justification" mean?

7. In the form for the Lord's Supper, we read in the confession of thanksgiving after the administration of the Lord's Supper this phrase: "being now justified in His blood." Does this only apply to those among God's children who have experienced justification subjectively in the court of their conscience?

10

Behold, I Stand at the Door and Knock...

The fourteenth chapter of Luke tells us that the Lord Jesus told a parable in response to someone's remark that "blessed is he that shall eat bread in the kingdom of God" (v. 15).

This parable is of great significance for those who are exercised with the Lord's Supper:

> A certain man made a great supper, and bade many: and sent his servant at supper time to say to them that were bidden, Come; for all things are now ready. And they all with one consent began to make excuse. The first said unto him, I have bought a piece of ground, and I must needs go and see it: I pray thee have me excused. And another said, I have bought five yoke of oxen, and I go to prove them: I pray thee have me excused. And another said, I have married a wife, and therefore I cannot come. So that servant came, and shewed his lord these things. Then the master of the house being angry said to his servant, Go out quickly into the streets and lanes of the city, and bring in hither the poor, and the maimed, and the halt, and the blind. And the servant said, Lord, it is done as thou hast commanded, and yet there is room. And the lord said unto the servant, Go out into the highways and hedges, and compel them to come in, that my house may be filled. For I say unto

you, That none of those men which were bidden shall taste of my supper (Luke 14:16–24).

I believe that the Lord Jesus used this parable to make clear that it is not sufficient for us merely to say, "Blessed is he that shall eat bread in the kingdom of God." It is true that such people are blessed, but what about you? Do you belong to those who eat bread in the kingdom of God? This is a matter of personal significance for each of us. How do we respond to the invitation from Him who is supreme wisdom Himself: "Whoso is simple, let him turn in hither: as for him that wanteth understanding, she saith to him, Come, eat of my bread, and drink of the wine which I have mingled. Forsake the foolish, and live; and go in the way of understanding" (Prov. 9:4–6)?

In this parable, the Lord Jesus also made very clear what the task of His servants is: they are to invite—even compel—sinners in His Name to partake of the meal that He has prepared and offers to them. The command "Compel them to come in" obviously does not mean that the invitees should be forced to come against their will; when they adamantly refuse to come and resist the sweetest and most urgent invitations, the responsibility rests with them rather than with the servants. Those who neither eat the Lord's bread nor drink of the wine will have to deal with the consequences.

The phrase "compel them to come in" can only refer to *verbal* compulsion. It means that with the greatest earnestness and utmost urgency (using appropriate words), the Lord's servants admonish sinners to partake of the Lord's invitation and accept His offer. If, however, they are neglectful of this compelling, then the responsibility for sinners not heeding this invitation rests with them.

So far, I have tried to make clear from Scripture why and for whom the Lord instituted His Supper. But I cannot and will not conclude this book without compelling you to partake of this meal which the Lord in His love and unfathomable goodness has prepared for the poor, contrite spirits who tremble at His Word (Isa. 66:2). For "when the needy seek Him, He will mercy show; yea, the weak and helpless shall His pity know; He will surely save them from oppression's might, for their lives are precious in His holy sight" (Psalter 200:2)!

The authors of the Heidelberg Catechism correctly concluded that the use of the sacraments belongs to the duties imposed by the fourth commandment. In response to the question, "What does God command in the fourth commandment?" they taught: "First, that the ministry of the gospel and the schools be maintained; and that I, especially on the Sabbath, that is, on the day of rest, diligently frequent the church of God, to hear His word, *to use the sacraments*...and yield myself to the Lord, to work by His Holy Spirit in me: and thus begin in this life the eternal Sabbath" (Heidelberg Catechism, Q. 103, emphasis mine).

We are not absolved from all responsibility by simply saying that the blessed are those who, as God's children, sit at the Lord's Table to eat His bread and drink His wine as signs and seals of His grace, love, and faithfulness. Serving God according to His precepts does not only include going to church to hear His Word, calling upon Him publicly, singing psalms to His honor, contributing financially to the maintenance of the church and the ministry of mercy, and receiving the sacrament of baptism; it also includes participation in the Lord's Supper according to the norms prescribed by Him in His Word. No one should be able to find any rest until he or she belongs to the multitude that keeps holyday (Ps. 42:4), showing forth the death of the Lord until He comes.

Practice confirms time and again that obedience to this command of love is contingent upon feeling a need for partaking of the Lord's Supper. This is not good! It is not our desire, but rather, His precept that should be our starting point for doing all that God commands us to do. Whoever challenges that, challenges God's precept, and this will yield spiritual barrenness.

My task, and that of all of God's servants, is to do what Jeremiah did (Jer. 17:16): as a shepherd moves his flock onward, we are likewise to insist upon obedience to the Lord's commands and "drive" sinners to the Lord—even when this is not appreciated. We cannot lead anyone to the Lord; only God's Spirit can accomplish this. We cannot move anyone to obey God's precepts; only the Lord can do so. But our responsibility is to "compel them to go in." The responsibility for not going in, and for not using what the Lord offers to us, rests with those who are invited. The responsibility of both the Lord's servants as well as the hearers of His Word is so great! May this, by the grace of God, lead us to humbly pray, "O God, be merciful to me, a sinner!" Upon such a supplication God shall be gracious indeed.

Just as the praying publican went to his home justified, so shall all be justified by God who penitently supplicate for grace, pleading on nothing else but His promise of forgiveness for Jesus' sake. God views such sinners as justified; the divine declaration of this truth is visibly signified and sealed by the Lord in the sacraments. By the administration of the sacraments, the God who cannot lie declares that all who penitently take refuge to the Savior shall find grace in His eyes—the Savior who said, "Come unto me all ye that labour and are heavy laden." They shall find rest for their troubled and restless souls when and how He appoints.

The Lord Jesus Christ once directed His apostle John to write a letter to the congregation of Laodicea. He testified to the Christians of Laodicea that He is "the Amen, the faithful and true witness, the beginning of the creation of God," and He had something very searching to say regarding the spiritual condition of these Christians. The One who knows our hearts and the secrets within, and before whom nothing in our heart and walk can be concealed, says, "I know thy works, that thou art neither cold nor hot: I would thou wert cold or hot. So then because thou art lukewarm, and neither cold nor hot, I will spue thee out of my mouth. Because thou sayest, I am rich, and increased with goods, and have need of nothing; and knowest not that thou art wretched, and miserable, and poor, and blind, and naked."

After the Savior had counseled these Christians "to buy of me gold tried in the fire, that thou mayest be rich; and white raiment, that thou mayest be clothed, and that the shame of thy nakedness do not appear; and anoint thine eyes with eyesalve, that thou mayest see," He proceeded to say to them, "As many as I love, I rebuke and chasten: be zealous therefore, and repent" (Rev. 3:14–19).

The nature of such zeal and repentance was communicated to these backslidden Christians in what Jesus already said, as well as by what followed the exhortation to be zealous and to repent: "Behold, I stand at the door, and knock: if any man hear my voice, and open the door, I will come in to him, and will sup with him, and he with me" (Rev. 3:20).

In this passage, the Lord Jesus uses a metaphor. As is true for all His parables, we must keep in mind that not every detail can be used as textual material to expound all the truths of the Holy Scriptures. If we fail to keep this in mind, we may end up making applications that are contradictory to the comprehensive context of the Lord's message in His Word.

Interpreting the words "Behold, I stand at the door, and knock: if any man hear my voice, and open the door, I will come in to him, and will sup with him, and he with me," in such a way that the Lord does not do anything unless we give Him the opportunity to do so is a wrong interpretation. If the works of the Lord were contingent upon our cooperation, not a single component of His counsel and redemptive plan would have been accomplished. No one of his own volition can cooperate with what is pleasing to the Lord. On the contrary, our natural tendency is to do nothing else but resist. If we read Scripture in its totality, we will find plainly that the Lord, in the accomplishment of His counsel and redemptive plan, works "in you both to will and to do of his good pleasure" (Phil. 2:13). He is and always will be the One who takes the initiative. "The carnal mind is enmity against God: for it is not subject to the law of God, neither indeed can be" (Rom. 8:7).

In Revelation (1:11, 17; 2:8; 22:13) we read that the Lord is the First and the Last. Were that not the case, no one would ever open the door of his heart when He knocked. No one would have ever bought of Him gold tried in the fire, white raiments, and eye-salve. No one would have ever anointed his eyes with this eye-salve and be zealous in the things of the Lord. No one would repent. No one would experience what the Lord says in Revelation 3:20: "I will come in to him, and will sup with him, and he with me."

However, in spite of our natural state of spiritual death and the remaining corruption of the regenerate, God has every right to address us with a variety of exhortations and invitations—exhortations and invitations that we are to consider *commands*. He created us in such a way that we were capable of doing all that He commands. He is not to be blamed for the fact that we are incapable of doing any good and are inclined toward all evil. Furthermore, in His condescending goodness and in response to our humble supplication, He will give us everything we need for obedience. All of God's precepts should stir us up to pray for that. It pleases Him when we ask Him to give us what we are missing (cf. Ezek. 36:37; Ps. 81:10).

All religious activity that is of our own devising is as much an abomination to the Lord as the absence of any activity. A worship of God according to our own norms displeases the Lord as much as no worship at all. It is His will that we would prayerfully, and in dependence upon Him, open the door upon which He is knocking. No one should have the audacity to try to neutralize the forceful appeal of the Lord's precepts, thereby rendering God's exhortations null and void. Anyone who argues thus will reap its bitter fruits. In His Word, the Lord refers to this as the hardening of the heart. "Who hath hardened himself against him, and hath prospered?" (Job 9:4). To whom has the Lord sworn that they will not enter into His rest? To the disobedient (Heb. 3:18–19). He therefore testifies, "To day if ye will hear his voice, harden not your heart" (Ps. 95:7–8).

We must not neglect or minimize any word the Lord prescribes. The nature of His exhortations and invitations is not such that those to whom they are addressed are without obligation; our failure to be exercised by them renders us guilty before God. The Lord considers this to be disobedience. He cannot and will not allow disobedience to His precepts to remain unpunished.

This also applies to the loving command which the Lord, prior to His departure, gave to His "congregation" at the institution of the Lord's Supper: "This do in remembrance of me."

Our input is entirely excluded in regard to *meriting* salvation. However, the Lord engages His children by His Word and Spirit when it comes to *partaking* of the salvation which Christ merited. He quickens them and stirs them up to be active. To accomplish this, He uses invitations such as, "Behold, I stand at the door, and knock: if any man hear my voice, and open the door, I will come in to him, and will sup with him, and he with me." With His loving commands, the Lord draws the hearts of His people to Himself, working in them "both to do and to will of his good pleasure." He *accomplishes* salvation and they *experience* salvation. Those who have been saved and who know this experientially will not be able to boast in anything but in the Lord. A true believer only humbly acknowledges that it was the Lord who, for the first time or by renewal, worked in him according to His own will.

"Behold, I stand at the door, and knock: if any man hear my voice, and open the door, I will come in to him, and will sup with him, and he with me," offers the very glad tidings of the gospel out of the mouth of the One who cannot lie. The Lord moved Isaiah to give the same gospel in the well-known words, "Come now, and let us reason together" (Isa. 1:18). The reasoning to which the Lord is referring in this text is not of such a nature that they who are troubled because of their sins, who penitently turn to Him for forgiveness and cleansing, and who sincerely desire to live according to His will have any reason to fear.

On the contrary! In the words directly following "Come now, let us reason together," the Lord directed Isaiah to emphasize this by saying, "Though your sins be as scarlet, they shall be as white as snow; though they be red like crimson, they shall be as wool" (Isa. 1:18). Immediately thereafter follows the pronouncement, "If ye be willing and obedient, ye shall eat the good of the land: but if ye refuse and rebel, ye shall be devoured with the sword: for the mouth of the Lord hath spoken it" (Isa. 1:19–20). Though the Lord uses different metaphors in Isaiah 1:18–20 and Revelation 3:20, the message is the same. What very glad tidings flowed from the mouth of Him of whom the poet testified that grace is poured forth into His lips (Ps. 45:1)! Isaiah also prophesied of this in chapter 61:1–3, saying,

The Spirit of the Lord GOD is upon me; because the

LORD hath anointed me to preach good tidings unto the
meek; he hath sent me to bind up the brokenhearted,
to proclaim liberty to the captives, and the opening
of the prison to them that are bound; to proclaim the
acceptable year of the LORD, and the day of vengeance
of our God; to comfort all that mourn; to appoint unto
them that mourn in Zion, to give unto them beauty
for ashes, the oil of joy for mourning, the garment
of praise for the spirit of heaviness; that they might
be called trees of righteousness, the planting of the
LORD, that he might be glorified.

The meek are those who fear Him and hope in His
mercy (Ps. 147:11). To such the Lord manifests His favor;
He takes pleasure in them. He does so by communicating
to them the promises of the gospel, visibly and tangibly
displayed in the sacraments, and personally favoring them
by granting His blessings. The blessings of the Lord, by
which all our physical and spiritual needs are met, make
us unspeakably rich. To be worthy of temporal and eternal
punishments, and then to be crowned with lovingkindness—to be worthy of being smitten, and then to be kissed
with the kisses of His mouth (Song 1:2)—this will satisfy
our heart and mouth with good things (Ps. 103:5). This
will cause us to remember His love more than wine (Song
1:4) and to love Him who loved us first and was crucified
for our sins, so that He could fill us with His blessings.

As stated earlier, the Lord Jesus speaks metaphori-
cally when He says, "I will come in to him, and will sup
with him, and he with me," depicting the totality of the
blessings He bestows on them who, in response to His
invitation, open the door of their heart.

These blessings include what He bestows upon the
poor and needy through the administration of the Lord's
Supper. He has promised that when two or three are gath-
ered in His name—among other things, to hear His Word

and to show forth His death—He shall be in the midst. He shall come to them and sup with them.

The Lord's Supper is like a door through which the Lord comes to His people in order to lead us into the green pastures of His covenant blessings (Ps. 23). His eternal good pleasure is visibly displayed before us to facilitate a better understanding of the promise of the gospel—the promise that He will graciously forgive sins and grant eternal life to all who humble themselves because of their sin and seek their righteousness and salvation outside of themselves in Christ Jesus (cf. Heidelberg Catechism, Q. 66, and the Forms for Baptism and the Lord's Supper).

When the Lord's Supper is administered, it is as if the Lord calls out to His people, saying, "Behold, I stand at the door, and knock: if any man hear my voice, and open the door, I will come in to him, and will sup with him, and he with me." He does so through the opened door to His pastures by way of this sacrament. It is an invitation extended to a people who are worthy of being spewed out of His mouth.

What a marvelous manifestation of the Lord's condescending goodness in His knocking at our door! Regretfully, we are not naturally inclined to sup with Him; Revelation 3:14–21 teaches us that the desire to sup with Christ can even be deficient in those who truly fear the Lord.

We misinterpret the mind of the Spirit if we think that the words addressed to the lukewarm Laodiceans are applicable to unconverted people only. Many eminent divines teach that Christ's metaphor is applicable to both the unconverted as well as those who have returned to the Bishop and Shepherd of their souls. Thus the metaphor does not only refer to the Lord supping with His people at His table; as long as we live in an unconverted state, and as long as we do not give heed to His invitation, He shall not sup with us—neither in the general sense of the word (i.e., the manifestation of His favor), nor in the specific sense of the word of supping with us during the Lord's Supper.

Both Word and sacraments are the means which the Lord uses to speak to the hearts of His people. When we partake of the Lord's Supper, the Lord wants us to enjoy the comfort expressed in the well-known words, "Comfort ye, comfort ye my people, saith your God. Speak ye comfortably to Jerusalem, and cry unto her, that her warfare is accomplished, that her iniquity is pardoned: for she hath received of the LORD's hand double for all her sins" (Isa. 40:1–2). The Lord instituted the Lord's Supper to turn His hand to the little ones, and He uses it to set the captives free. It is, however, upon the obedient use of His divinely ordained means of grace that He is pleased to free them. Standing fast "in the liberty wherewith Christ hath made us free" (Gal. 5:1) and walking in the light of His countenance, they thus "give ear" to His gracious overtures.

Satan will leave no stone unturned to keep us from the use of these means. By his whispers and accomplices, he is always out to persuade you that these means and invitations are not intended for you. They are for others. You are far too…—you finish the sentence! Due to our unbelieving disposition, we are too inclined to listen to his "instruction," and this has wretched consequences for us.

The Lord wills that we respond to His invitation, in total dependence upon His Spirit and in accord with His Word, by humbly making use of what He gave us in His Son, His Word, and the sacraments. If our disregard for the Lord's revealed will is motivated by our own condition, our own opinion, or that of others (whoever they may be), the Lord calls this a hardening of ourselves. This is an expression of unbelief and disobedience, and it will cause us to remain in darkness.

It is good that we pray continually, "Draw me, and we shall run after thee" (Song 1:4). The Lord says, "I will yet for this be enquired of by the house of Israel, to do it for them" (Ezek. 36:37). However, it is not good when such petitions are not accompanied by a proper use of the means of grace.

If we only dared to partake of the Lord's Supper as a divinely ordained means of grace after determining with absolute certainty that the Lord is at work in us savingly, we would be reversing God's established order. We would not be acting in accord with God's revealed will; He ordained the use of the sacraments in order to give assurance. Normally, such assurance is not obtained prior to, but rather, by the use thereof. The Lord, by means of the sacraments, desires to assure His people that they, for Christ's sake alone, are incorporated into the covenant of grace and have found grace in His eyes. It pleases Him to use the sacraments to assure His people that they are His and He is theirs, and, by His Spirit, to lead them believingly and humbly to concur with the bride in the Song of Solomon, "My beloved is mine, and I am his" (2:16).

Since the Lord knows that some of His people often dare not number themselves among the elect who have been incorporated into the essence of the covenant of grace (this being such an extraordinary privilege), He comes to their aid through the visible, tangible instruction given in the sacraments. By these signs and seals of His "hearty love and faithfulness," He is pleased to grant His people such assurance.

Although some of those who take refuge in Him often fail to believe they have found grace in God's eyes (being unable to discern the evidences of this with perfect clarity), it is nevertheless the Lord's will that they would partake of His Supper in order that their weak faith might be strengthened. God's Word teaches that "him that worketh not, but believeth on him that justifieth the ungodly, his faith is counted for righteousness" (Rom. 4:5). As proof of this, the Lord gave Abraham the sign of circumcision as a seal of the righteousness of faith. This sign sealed that he was righteous in the eyes of God for Christ's sake.

The Passover was also a sign and seal of the righteousness of faith. They who believingly took refuge in the blood of the paschal lamb would be assured that God graciously would pass by when the angel of death would come, and they would be spared from His wrath.

The Lord gave Holy Baptism and the Lord's Supper to the New Testament church. These sacraments signify and seal the same matter as did circumcision and the Passover, but without blood. By giving them the broken bread and the poured out wine, the Lord proclaims to His people, "Be not unbelieving but believing, for this is My body which is broken for you; this is My blood which is shed for you."

Who are the worthy partakers of the Lord's Table? Not they who deem themselves worthy, but they whom God deems worthy to partake of the table of His Son, Jesus Christ. And who does He deem worthy? The authors of the Lord's Supper Form answered this so beautifully: They who are unworthy in themselves, who mourn the fact that they do not have a perfect faith and who do not give themselves to serve God with that zeal as they are bound, who grieve over and are troubled about finding nothing in themselves but death, who cannot save themselves, and who therefore take refuge in Christ for salvation.

Granted, no one may pretend to be something he is not. He who does so will "eat and drink damnation to himself, not discerning the Lord's body." But if you are not a stranger of what has been discussed and you do not partake of the Lord's Supper, you will be grieving the Lord. You deny Him who purchased us with His blood. Such failure to partake is wrong—however understandable the hesitation may be, being fearful of eating and drinking damnation to ourselves. Our refusal shortchanges the Lord and ourselves. However great the temptation may be to stay home when the Lord's Supper is administered, or to refrain from partaking to avoid internal strife, such disobedience to the Lord's command of love will generate a different strife—a strife, as experience has proven, that will often be greater and more intense. Many of God's children have wept as they left the church building after failing to acknowledge publicly that the Lord Jesus was precious to them.

Do not seek worthiness for partaking of the Lord's Supper where worthiness is not to be found. Worthiness is rooted in the Inviter and His invitation, not in the invitee. Worthy partakers have no worthiness in themselves but derive their freedom to respond to His invitation from His command.

In *Wat Willem Teelinck zegt over de zelf-beproeving tot het Heilig Avondmaal* [What Willem Teelinck says regarding self-examination for the Lord's Supper], we read, "You need to know that no one has any inherent worthiness to approach to the Lord's Table. All of our worthiness proceeds from the fact that our Lord Jesus Christ has deemed us worthy to be invited to His table. If, therefore, we gratefully accept this invitation and prepare ourselves in accord with His will, we shall be welcome as His guests and He will deem us worthy partakers of His Table."

Later we read, "He who is aware of his spiritual deficiency and weakness, must not permit himself to refrain from coming to the Lord's Table. On the contrary, this is precisely what should stimulate you all the more to partake, for this table has in fact been set for those who feel their deficiencies and desire to be strengthened. As long as your heart is upright before the Lord, and you sincerely intend to forsake and battle sin, you must come to the Lord's Table for that very reason, so that you may be strengthened in your good intentions and the spiritual battle you are waging."

Finally, Teelinck says, "Therefore, though it may perhaps be that you cannot surely believe, and thus without any doubt, that your sins are forgiven and that there is healing for your spiritual maladies, as long as you do hunger and thirst for this, you will be a welcome guest at the Lord's Table. We are dealing with a gracious Lord who will neither break the bruised reed nor quench the smoking flax—yes, who has promised that He will satisfy those who sincerely hunger and thirst for these things" (Matt. 5:6).

When the woman with the issue of blood took refuge to Jesus by touching the hem of His garment, she experienced deliverance from her misery. Did this woman, when she pushed herself through the crowd and touched His garment, know that it was the Lord who drew her to Himself? I believe not. And yet, He did! Having found no healing from other physicians, and taking refuge as an unworthy, miserable, and helpless one to Him who alone could help, she was drawn by the Father. As the Lord Jesus said, "No one can come to me, except the Father which hath sent me, draw him" (John 6:44). Subsequently, the woman would have readily acknowledged and confessed that, if the Lord had not drawn her to Himself, she would have never come to Him.

We are not doing ourselves any favors by not availing ourselves of what the Lord invites us to partake of. "Behold, I stand at the door and knock," speaks the Savior. "If any man hear my voice, and open the door, I will come in to him, and will sup with him, and he with me." Hear Him who says, "Ho, every one that thirsteth, come ye to the waters, and he that hath no money; come ye, buy, and eat; yea, come, buy wine and milk without money and without price. Wherefore do ye spend money for that which is not bread? and your labour for that which satisfieth not? hearken diligently unto me, and eat ye that which is good, and let your soul delight itself in fatness. Incline your ear, and come unto me: hear, and your soul shall live; and I will make an everlasting covenant with you, even the sure mercies of David" (Isa. 55:1–3).

"Who hath hardened himself against him, and hath prospered?" (Job 9:4). The Lord Jesus Himself declares, "And let him that is athirst come. And whosoever will, let him take the water of life freely" (Rev. 22:17b). "I will give unto him that is athirst of the fountain of the water of life freely" (Rev. 21:6). To the Samaritan woman He said, and thus also to us, "But whosoever drinketh of the water that I shall give him shall never thirst; but the water that I shall give him shall be in him a well of water springing up into everlasting life" (John 4:14).

The Lord will confirm these very glad tidings and this glorious divine promise for His Name's sake. May the Lord so bless these words that they lead to humble and yet bold and joyful obedience to His loving command, "This do in remembrance of me." May He grant that, in harmony with the precepts of His Word, we would often practice what is written in Psalter 426:7 (Ps. 116),

What shall I render to Jehovah now
For all the riches of His consolation?
With joy I'll take the cup of His salvation,
And call upon His Name with thankful vow.

"Behold, I stand at the door and knock. If any man hear my voice, and open the door, I will come in to him, and will sup with him, and he with me" (Rev. 3:20).

Discussion Questions

1. Who defines our worthiness to partake of the Lord's Supper?

2. From where does this worthiness proceed? From us? From something that is of us? From something we have accomplished?

3. What are the causes and consequences of keeping the door closed on which the Lord is knocking?

4. What does the opening of the door, referred to in Revelation 3:20, consist of?

5. Is Peter's denial on par with not partaking of the Lord's Supper by those whom the Lord commanded to eat of His bread and drink of His wine in remembrance of Him?

6. What blessings will the Lord bestow upon those who show forth His death until He comes?

ALSO BY ARIE ELSHOUT

A Helping Hand
Hardback, 125 pages

"The writer addresses you in this book as one who identifies himself with you in your tribulations. The Lord gave him this grace. It was the desire of my friend Arie Elshout to remove the wrong idea that a converted person, and even a minister of the gospel, cannot come into a state of deep depression, be haressed with thoughts that there is no God, or even for a time lose his right mind."

—CORNELIS HARINCK

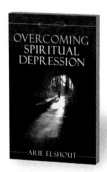

Overcoming Spiritual Depression
Paperback, 115 pages

"Arie Elshout's *Overcoming Spiritual Depression* is a treasure of pastoral counsel. Reminiscent as it is of A. W. Pink's *Elijah* and Martyn Lloyd-Jones's *Spiritual Depression,* Elshout employs the life of Elijah to cover a variety of related themes. Always sensitive to the complexities of the human spirit, this book manages to be profoundly insightful, thoroughly biblical, and theologically astute all at once. For Christians caught in Bunyan's Castle of Giant Despair, this book is bound to provide a key that will aid in the process of recovery. Thoroughly recommended."

—DEREK W. H. THOMAS

OTHER RHB BOOKS OF INTEREST

The Earnest Communicant

Ashton Oxenden

Introduced by Cornelis Pronk

Paperback, 48 pages
ISBN 978-1-60178-069-0

"The blessings of coming to the Lord's Table are beyond calculation! They seem to increase with our desire to know Christ better and to live in ongoing communion with Him. Although we often feel poorly prepared to meet Him, He comes to meet us. But we long to be better prepared to welcome Him.

"For those who do, *The Earnest Communicant* will be our great help. Gently and graciously it will lead you to see your need afresh—but also to see that Jesus Christ is more full of grace than you are of sin. Ashton Oxenden knew this well and teaches us afresh that, at the Lord's Supper, Christ stands at the door and knocks. If anyone opens the door, He will come in and share the supper with them. Our Lord Jesus Christ welcomes and receives sinners at His Table!"

—SINCLAIR B. FERGUSON

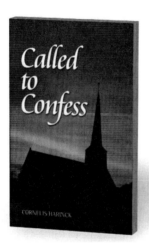

Called to Confess

Cornelis Harinck

Paperback, 138 pages
ISBN 1-892777-28-2

"How can we preserve the important link between public profession of faith and the Lord's Supper without encouraging presumptuous attendance at the Lord's Table? How can we guard against reducing public profession of faith to a mere confession of truth? How can we maintain the proper relationship between baptism and a baptized person's responsibility to profess faith in Christ and show forth His death in the midst of the congregation? How can we encourage every confessing member to engage in thorough self-examination before coming to the Lord's Table?

"Rev. Cor Harinck deals with these issues thoroughly and with maturity born of forty years of pastoral ministry. He interacts profitably with the biblical, confessional, and historical data on confession of faith. Pastors, office-bearers, teachers, and young people should carefully study this book."

—JOEL R. BEEKE AND BARTEL ELSHOUT

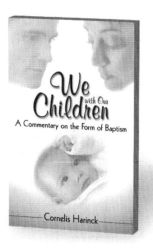

We with Our Children:
**A Commentary on the
Form of Baptism**

Cornelis Harinck

Paperback, 200 pages
ISBN 978-1-892777-92-8

"*We with Our Children* provides an enlightening, balanced, and detailed exposition of the Dutch Reformed 'Form for the Administration of Baptism.' It guides us through all the potential landmines associated with baptism and provides us with a rich, edifying treatment of infant baptism. Every office-bearer and parent should read this book."

—JOEL R. BEEKE

"Cor Harinck has provided a clear and well-written exposition of the Dutch Reformed 'Form for the Administration of Baptism.' He demonstrates that the authors of this form had a masterful grasp of Reformed covenant theology—an understanding that needs to be recovered. Reading this book yields a genuine appreciation for the fact that this form is a jewel among the Reformed liturgical forms."

—BARTEL ELSHOUT

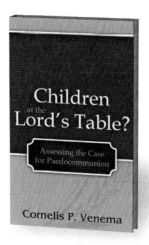

Children at the Lord's Table?
Assessing the Case for Paedocommunion

Cornelis P. Venema

Hardcover, 200 pages
ISBN 978-1-60178-059-1

"Dr. Venema has done a great service for the Reformed churches in presenting a clear compelling biblical case for our historic practice regarding admission to the Lord's Table. For about thirty-five years now, proponents of paedocommunion have been producing papers, articles, and monographs stating their historical and exegetical case(s) for paedocommunion. They have argued that to be consistent with our covenant theology we need to practice infant or young child communion. In this carefully and charitably articulated book, Venema shows why their arguments are not persuasive, and counters with historical, confessional, and exegetical support for what has been the official public theology and practice of the Protestant churches from their inception."

—J. LIGON DUNCAN III
Senior Minister of First Presbyterian,
Jackson, Mississippi